FIX IT

MW01274901

MANAGING
ANGER AND
IRRITATION

A TOOLKIT
FOR MEN

Kim Richardson
STROUD COUNSELLING

MANAGING ANGER AND IRRITATION
A toolkit for men

First published in 2010
by Stroud Counselling
41 London Road, Stroud
Gloucestershire GL5 2AJ

Cover and interior design
by Paola Costamagna

ISBN 978-0-9564076-0-3 (pbk)
ISBN 978-0-9564076-1-0 (pdf)

Permission to reproduce the Novaco Provocation
Inventory on page 22 has been applied for.

To my clients, who have taught me so much.

I welcome comments and feedback on this book.
Please email me at kim@stroudcounselling.net

CONTENTS

Series preface iv

Introduction vii

1 Key skills 1

2 Own up – you're angry 17

3 Understand your anger 30

4 Take control 49

5 Challenge your beliefs 61

6 Deal with irritation and frustration 80

7 Stop taking things personally 98

8 Be assertive 111

9 De-stress yourself 131

Appendix 1 My anger toolkit 148

Appendix 2 To the partner in your life 149

Appendix 3 Further help 151

Appendix 4 Challenge checklist 154

Appendix 5 Ten key assertiveness techniques 155

SERIES PREFACE

Why a series of self-help books for men?

My experience in counselling men over many years tells me that men are missing out. It tells me that we have particular concerns and needs. That we can look at issues in ways that women don't. That we think and talk about them – if at all – in particular ways. That we often find it hard, even in these enlightened times, to face our emotions. That we can easily feel threatened at the very suggestion of being needy.

For all these reasons I decided to put together a set of resources that men can access, which are written by men and aimed at men.

Each book tackles an issue that concerns men, such as anger management, relationship problems or assertiveness. Yes, most of these issues concern women as well, but often in a different way.

I have found that explaining the cycles or patterns of behaviour that we can get into as men is often the starting point to getting on top of it. Men like to feel in control. (*Not* feeling in control is at the root of a lot of our problems.) That's why a straightforward explanation early on can reassure us. If an idea makes sense, it seems more possible to let it in and give it a chance.

In my consulting room I have a large whiteboard and a pad of A3 paper. As clients talk me through the latest flare up, or last week's crisis, I sketch out for them what is going on. Even better, *they* sketch it out. They have found this so helpful, that this visual approach is a feature I am including in the Fix It books.

Men like problem solving. We prefer to see an issue as something to sort out than as something to sit with, endlessly discuss and meditate on, explore at all sorts of levels of feeling. I am not saying that either of these approaches is better than the other. But if men are wired up to consider an important issue in a particular way, then it makes sense to give them the tools to do it in that way.

That's why these books are essentially toolkits. They set out what a problem may look like, then provide you with the tools to deal with it. The aim is straightforward and practical: problem ●●●> solution. The tools that you use may be new ones, but they will be essential companions in the future so that you can keep on top of the problem.

The emphasis is on the practical throughout. Men like to get on with things, try things out, see things in action. In my work with men I try to appreciate this by getting them to make an actual change in their lives, however small, early on in the process. It gives them a sense of control in an area where they are feeling trapped or powerless.

The approach is practical in other ways too. The basic theory or model underlying these toolkits is cognitive behavioural therapy, or CBT. (I promise not to use these words again!) One key principle in this model is that it is helpful to form ideas, or hypotheses, about how things could be different in our lives. We can then test these ideas out in practice, learn from them, and end up acting in ways that help us rather than hold us back.

This is a scientific approach that suits many men. We are used to trial and error, to learning what works, then copying it. We don't get bogged down in theory, any more than we (notoriously) don't start a construction job by reading the user manual.

So these books are about action. But not just about action. Because we are more than just acting beings – we are also thinking beings. And a key factor in getting us into trouble, and keeping us there, is our thinking patterns. That's why a lot of the work I do with men addresses how they think about the issues that consume them. And that's why there is an emphasis on thinking skills in these books.

To sum up, the series is based on two key beliefs:

- That men are different – they think about things differently and cope differently with challenges

- That men are also practical and resourceful, if only they had the understanding and the tools to do the job.

FIX IT gives you the tools. Now it's over to you to make your life better.

Kim Richardson

INTRODUCTION

Why am I reading this book?

Anger is associated with a range of mental, physical and social problems, including depression, self-harm, strokes, heart disease, stress, social withdrawal and relationship problems. For men in particular, anger can result in aggressive behaviour. Men are less able to recognise and talk about angry behaviour in themselves or others, even though they are much more likely to worry about the strength of their angry feelings. ('Boiling Point', Mental Health Foundation report, 2008)

Yet anger itself may not be the problem, as anger is a basic and vital human emotion. It's confusing, isn't it?

So you could be reading this book to answer any number of questions:

- Why do I get so angry?
- How can I learn to recognise anger and express it more appropriately?
- Is it better to let my angry feelings out, or keep them in?
- Is being angry always a bad thing?
- How did I become so irritable?
- What can I do to kick this habit?
- How can I communicate what I want in a way that is safe?
- How does stress contribute to my anger?
- Other people make me angry, don't they?

- How long will my partner put up with me being like this?
- How can I pull myself back from the brink of violence?
- Is being so angry actually bad for my health?
- How can I take control when I feel so out of control?

Managing Anger and Irritation: A Toolkit for Men explains the cycles or patterns of behaviour that angry men can easily get into. It then presents the tools that you can use to turn those cycles round. Whether you are stressed, depressed, unassertive or just plain overreactive, the emphasis is on taking effective action, based on sound and helpful thinking patterns. By doing this you will soon gain a sense of control in an area where at the moment you may be feeling trapped or powerless.

How should I use this book?

Reading Chapter 1 is essential. It explains some key skills and approaches that underlie the whole of the rest of the book.

Managing Anger and Irritation continues by explaining what anger is, how to judge whether you have an anger problem, and how to understand your own personal patterns of anger. A central emphasis is on how you interpret situations – this is where utilising your thinking skills comes into its own. The final chapters discuss three key issues that often underlie men's anger problems – sensitivity to criticism, unassertiveness and stress.

In more detail, here is a road map of the book's chapters:

In chapter 1 (Key skills) you are introduced to some key skills that you will need to take control of your anger problem. The skill of understanding helps you work out exactly how the anger cycle maintains itself. The skill of commitment means taking responsibility for what is yours – and that you are part of the solution. The skill of gathering information turns us into scientists of our own anger. The skill of thinking realistically and helpfully is absolutely key. The skill of taking action means practising new habits and learning from setbacks.

In chapter 2 (Own up – you're angry) you are going to discover whether you really are angry. You will explore what makes anger a problem in your life – what its impact is on you, your friends, your colleagues and your family. You will also learn why it is so easy to deny that you play the key part in this problem, and explode some myths that men hold that help them deny responsibility. Finally you will learn how to make an act of commitment to change.

In chapter 3 (Understand your anger) you will learn in more detail what anger actually is, the different parts of the anger process, and how you can intervene in each of these parts. You will identify the triggers for your own anger, and understand the underlying factors that can feed into us being angry. You will think about your own distinctive pattern of anger, and learn whether suppressing anger is better than expressing it. Finally you will learn that one major goal is to turn the heat down on your anger.

In chapter 4 (Take control) you will practise using some emergency tools to prevent you tipping over from anger into rage or violence. You will explore how talking to someone or throwing yourself into a different activity can help you let off steam. You will find ways of avoiding things that trigger your anger, and explore the role of drink and drugs in the cycle of anger.

In chapter 5 (Challenge your beliefs) you will learn how thinking errors are a major cause of men getting angry, and so how catching your thoughts and changing them is a key way of turning the heat down on your anger. You will also question some of the unwritten rules or assumptions that men have about their anger, and explore how you can use visualisation or imagery to reduce your anger.

In chapter 6 (Deal with irritation and frustration) you learn how to manage irritation and frustration. You discover how 'low frustration tolerance' (LFT) causes anger, and identify the thinking errors that lie behind LFT. You learn a simple way of problem-solving as an alternative to worrying or being a victim. You learn how anger is linked to depression, and how to relieve yourself of angry feelings left over from the past.

In chapter 7 (Stop taking things personally) you will learn how taking things personally, fearing criticism and 'loss of face' lie behind a lot of men's anger. You will identify the common thinking errors that contribute to you over-personalising. You will explore how low self-esteem links directly to anger, and what you can do to address this problem more effectively. You will also tackle the issue of perfectionism and 'fear of failure'.

In chapter 8 (Be assertive) you will learn how being passive often results in anger and aggression, and you will explore how to be assertive instead in your communication and behaviour. You discover a simple three-step model of assertiveness, and explore how best to deal with criticism and conflict.

In chapter 9 (De-stress yourself) you learn about the links between anger and stress. You explore how attention to relaxation, exercise and diet alters your physical responses to stress. You learn how to change your behavioural responses to stress, focusing on procrastination and work-life balance. And you learn how to think in a more helpful and effective way when under stress.

In each chapter I have tried to break up the text so that it doesn't look like a novel. There is a clear statement of aims at the start. There are 'case study' boxes, which are loosely based on real situations that I have worked with in my practice. These show in detail what can actually happen – how men can both get into trouble and out of it – and help to pin down the ideas through examples. There are also 'Do it!' boxes, which are important ways of getting you to take steps to make changes.

Do not skip the Do it! boxes. You cannot get on top of your anger through understanding alone. You also need to make changes and take action. You need to practise doing and thinking things differently. The activities in these boxes have been written to help you do that. They are not optional extras!

Each chapter ends with a learning log to help you record what you have learnt and how this helps you move towards your goal. There is also a summary of the tools you have used, and that you need to use, to move you on. The 'copymaster' icons refer to the photocopiable worksheets available in the accompanying **Copymaster Resource Book.**

An appendix is addressed to the 'partner in your life'. It may be that she or he bought this book for you in the first place. So your partner – whoever that may be – very often wants you to get on top of your problems as well. For their sake as well as yours. This appendix aids that process.

The book also includes a short section on getting further help. This is important. We can manage some issues on our own. Men are capable of turning even huge problems round. But often our own resources are not enough. And it would be arrogant for me to assume that reading a book like this will always make all the difference. In some cases it is vital to access further help – either through other written or audio resources, or through organisations, or by going to a counsellor or therapist.

But let's end on a more optimistic note. You have identified a problem – that's why you are reading this book. You are interested in seeing what you can do to solve it. That means you are already taking some responsibility for the problem, and that you are on the way to committing yourself to turning it round. These are huge steps *that you have already taken.*

Now take some more.

1 | KEY SKILLS

AIMS

To introduce some important skills that you will need as you read and act on the advice in this book. These are:

- Understanding
- Commitment
- Gathering information
- Thinking
- Taking action

The skills listed above aren't new. We practise them thousands of times every day. But sometimes we need to revisit these skills in the light of particular problems. It is the obvious things that can drop off the radar, simply because we take them for granted. These skills are absolutely key to the rest of the book. That's why it is so vital that you do not skip this chapter.

UNDERSTANDING

As men, we place a great amount of emphasis on understanding. It makes us feel on top of things. It means we can give an opinion about it – often a very firmly expressed opinion. Understanding a problem allows us to take further steps towards solving it.

Often men do not understand why they get angry. It is difficult to see what their anger is in response to, and how to deal with it. They are consumed by feelings that seem to come from nowhere, yet have a terrible effect. When men 'lose it' they also lose the capacity to think clearly and act effectively.

So their lack of understanding can be an important factor in feeling insecure and out of control. Which contributes to their anger. It's a vicious circle that looks like this:

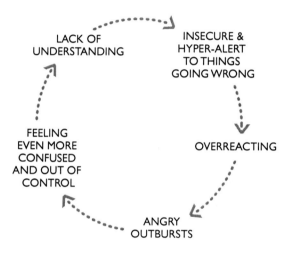

Fig. 1.1 The vicious circle of confusion and anger

CASE STUDY

Ben prided himself on keeping cool and calm. He knew from experience as a child what damage an angry man, like his father, could do. So he was devastated when he found himself 'blowing up' at his wife, apparently at the most trivial of things. This knocked his self-image so much that he became more and more on edge when they were together. It was like treading on eggshells. He desperately didn't want to lose his cool, but found as his confusion increased he was more and more inclined to explode. In the end he couldn't trust himself to stay with his wife, so he left her.

So understanding anger is important – what sets it off, why we respond in particular ways, what the actual effects are of anger, and so on.

Getting to grips with these issues is the subject of the next chapter. But understanding doesn't stop there. You can read other books. You can research the subject on the internet. You can share your thoughts and experiences with other men, especially if they are people whose views you respect. (If they are just going to reinforce your prejudices, then forget it.)

Choose an issue that is troubling you right now. It doesn't have to be about anger. Now discuss this issue with someone you trust. Be as objective as possible – try to discover what exactly is going on. After your discussion, ask yourself: 'What have I understood about it that I didn't understand before? How does this help me to take effective action?'

For some men, understanding a problem also means understanding *why* they are like they are. There is a historical angle to the problem which really niggles them. They might be aware of some key experiences in their life, or some key relationships they have had, which seem to be relevant but they don't really know how. They see things like this:

KEY EXPERIENCES IN THE PAST

PRESENT CYCLE OF DIFFICULTY

Fig. 1.2 Relating the past to the present

Making these links can be very helpful for some people. If you make a link with the past, however, try to use it in a positive way. You can *make* a link in order to *break* the link. To see this in action, read the case study below.

CASE STUDY

After some thought and discussion, Ben (see page 2 above) came to link his behaviour with his childhood. When he was young he was too frightened to be angry in case it was as destructive as his father's anger was. One result was that he became terrified of getting angry with his wife. But instead of saying, 'So I'm just going to end up like my father' he now chose to think more constructively: 'That explains why I am so nervous about being angry. But I can do things differently. As long as I turn the heat of my anger down, I can learn that it's OK to be angry at times.' Ben adjusted his self-image by coming to accept that he wasn't as cool as he thought – and that this was OK.

What is even more important than understanding the past is understanding how the past has shaped your assumptions or belief system. Ben couldn't change the *facts* of his past. But what he could change was how he *responded* to the past. This set up a new pattern of thinking and behaviour:

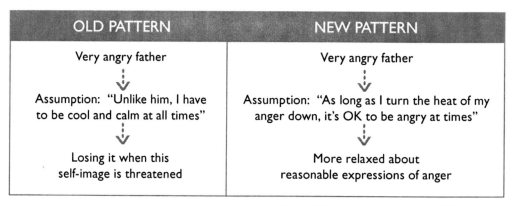

OLD PATTERN	NEW PATTERN
Very angry father	Very angry father
Assumption: "Unlike him, I have to be cool and calm at all times"	Assumption: "As long as I turn the heat of my anger down, it's OK to be angry at times"
Losing it when this self-image is threatened	More relaxed about reasonable expressions of anger

Fig. 1.3 Responding to the past in different ways

We will talk more about the importance of assumptions later on.

Don't get hung up on the past. Don't even feel you have to understand it in order to make changes in the present. It's more important to notice what you are doing now, take responsibility for that, and make effective changes.

COMMITMENT

Understanding is helpful, but it is not enough. There also needs to be a commitment to change. This means several things:

- A commitment to take responsibility for what is yours
  – *that you are part of the problem*
- A commitment to take effective action to turn the situation round
  – *that you are part of the solution.*

Both of these commitments, or promises to yourself, are important. Some men focus on the first and neglect the second. They beat themselves up for their behaviour and don't allow themselves to move on, or to use their resources to make positive changes. This is hugely destructive. They don't benefit, nor do those people who may be the objects of their anger.

Other men neglect the first commitment and thereby get stuck on the second. They think, 'I can make changes here, but hey, why should I? I've got every right to be angry.' Basically it's all the other person's fault, or the fault of the world, or of things in general. These men don't make changes either – but out of misguidedness and resentment. This is equally destructive and self-defeating.

One characteristic of anger, at least among men, is that it is easy to blame others for our anger. It is easy not to accept responsibility for our own reactions. So it is easy to deny that we are even in the wrong – that there is anything we ought to be doing differently. This is such an important side effect of anger that we look at it in more detail in chapter 2.

Making a commitment to change is one thing. Maintaining it is another. After an initial flush of success or enthusiasm comes the hard graft of trying things out, testing deeply held beliefs, moving out of your comfort zone.

It is important that you encourage yourself while you are on this challenging journey. One way of doing this is to note what you are learning and how this is moving you in the direction you want to go. That is why each chapter ends with a page where you can record these thoughts.

Even more effective is to keep a separate log, or brief journal, of your learning. It can be as simple as this:

DATE	WHAT HAPPENED	WHAT I LEARNED
6 June	Blew up at work again	I noticed that I was really stressed before I lost it – tight chested and breathing fast. But taking a few deep breaths helped calm me down
7 June	Spoke to manager about shift problem	I thought he'd be dismissive and I'd get mad. But he actually listened. Addressing the issue stopped me building up resentment

Fig. 1.4 Example of learning log

GATHERING INFORMATION

The learning log brings us neatly to another of the key skills you will use in fixing your anger problem. I will be asking you to note things down, to record evidence, to make statements of intent.

Before you groan and turn the page, let me emphasise the three huge benefits that making records and logging information brings: motivation, evidence and understanding.

Motivation. Change often occurs slowly, and in small steps. So it's easy to overlook small but significant steps that you are taking towards your goal. Recording these steps makes them more real. You cannot forget or dismiss them, because they are there in black and white. So recording what you are doing is itself a tool in driving you onwards.

Studies have shown that writing increases commitment. This is partly because it is so active. The process involved in getting your thoughts from brain to pen (or keyboard) engages and involves you at many subtle levels. And moving your hand across the page is taking action. Anything that increases commitment in this way will direct you more quickly towards your goal.

Say to yourself: 'I commit to getting on top of my anger problem.' Say this three times to yourself.
Now write the sentence down on a piece of paper. Write it three times.
What difference do you notice? Which is more powerful?

Evidence. As you will see, the method you will use to address your anger problem is evidence-based. This means you will be looking very closely at what goes on when you get angry – the triggers, what you are thinking, what you are doing, what the effect is etc. You will use this evidence to make an assessment of where you could be going wrong, and how you could intervene to speak or act less angrily.

You will then need to record what happens when you make changes. How can you use evidence accurately unless you collect the evidence accurately in the first place? Scientists may dream up theories in their sleep, but when it comes to the lab they gather the data and test the theory rigorously. You are going to become a scientist of anger.

CASE STUDY

Rod thought that he always got most angry whenever something went wrong – a scratch on his car, the photocopier not working, screwing up on a DIY job. But when he made a record of his anger 'triggers' he found that he could often cope very well with things going wrong. So what made the difference? The key factor that came to light was his belief that he would be blamed or criticised in some way for the mishap. Identifying this allowed him to address the root of the problem – his over-sensitivity.

Understanding. Recording data also hugely aids understanding. We can see what exactly is happening – it is there in front of our eyes. That means we can be more objective about the problem, and begin to address it more rationally and less emotionally.

This is particularly important with anger, because when we are extremely angry we have lost control. This is both frightening and dangerous. By recording, we observe what is going on. This distances us in a subtle but significant way from the turmoil of thoughts and feelings. This in turn allows us to get on top of our thoughts and feelings, instead of the thoughts and feelings running us. We gain more control through our understanding.

Buy an A5 notebook or ringbound book. Make it your personal logbook. If you live or work in a paper-free environment then open a spreadsheet file on your computer instead.

THINKING

Or rather – thinking straight. We all think, after all, don't we? But we often think in ways that are unrealistic, unhelpful, illogical, plain stupid.

Why does this matter? Because the thoughts that we have and the beliefs that we hold play the single biggest part in the feelings that we feel – including anger. In short:

THOUGHTS ⋯⟩ FEELINGS

Fig. 1.5 Our thoughts influence our feelings

This is a basic finding of psychology, with profound implications for how we feel and act. But it needs some explanation – see the case study.

CASE STUDY

Six businessmen are all trying to work on the morning train. They don't know each other. Two young men sitting immediately behind them are laughing and joking loudly. After ten minutes, each of the six has a particular feeling.

Sacha: Extreme anger

Paul: Amusement

Alan: Mild annoyance, then calm

Ashwani: Goodwill, relaxed

Peter: Inadequacy, regret

Alex: Anxiety

What caused these feelings? Most people say, 'The young men laughing and joking.' But that's illogical. How can one event cause so many different feelings at the same time?

Instead, it is more accurate to say that the laughing and joking *triggered* the men's reactions. It was the 'activating event'. But it triggered very different reactions. Why?

Because of the different thoughts and beliefs that each of the businessmen had. This is the missing link. Their thoughts and beliefs are the true cause of their feelings.

Here is the full story:

Sacha
They are behaving disgracefully. People like that should be thrown off.
...> EXTREME ANGER

Paul
It's actually very funny what they are saying, though it's interrupting my work
...> AMUSEMENT

Alan
I can't concentrate, so I'll block them out with my iPod.
...> MILD ANNOYANCE, THEN CALM

Ashwani
It's nice to see young people enjoying themselves. My work can wait
...> GOODWILL, RELAXED

Peter
I never have fun like that with my mates. What's wrong with me?
...> INADEQUACY, REGRET

Alex
I'm never going to finish this report now – this is disastrous.
...> ANXIETY

Fig. 1.6 What the businessmen are thinking and feeling

We can now construct a straightforward formula to describe this whole process. A trigger or activating event (A) plus a set of thoughts or beliefs (B) has certain consequences (C):

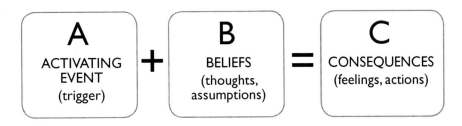

A		B		C
ACTIVATING EVENT (trigger)	**+**	BELIEFS (thoughts, assumptions)	**=**	CONSEQUENCES (feelings, actions)

Fig. 1.7 The A B C formula

The consequences are in the first place our feelings. And by feelings we mean both emotional reactions and physical sensations (a rise in blood pressure, tense shoulders etc). But because feelings are powerful things, we act on them. These actions are also consequences of our beliefs. Here is the full picture for Sacha:

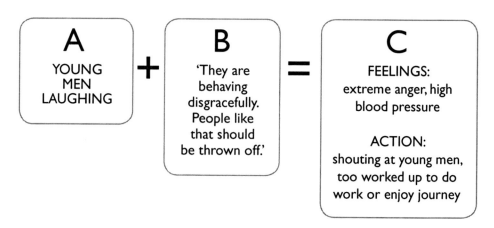

Fig. 1.8 Sacha's thinking/feeling process

Of course this is a simplification. The consequences for Sacha don't stop here. As a result of losing it he will have further thoughts, such as 'Why can't I control myself?' and 'How am I going to get any useful work done now?' These will result in further feelings, such as guilt and anxiety. And so the cycle continues. And deepens.

During the course of this book you will learn to take control over your thoughts. We actually generate all our own thoughts, even if it seems like they come out of the blue. So if we produce them in the first place, it is also possible to examine them, challenge them, adjust them, replace them. The benefits of this are enormous. Instead of being run by our feelings, we can think in a realistic and helpful way to take charge of our feelings. If you like being in control – and most men do – then getting on top of your thinking is a key tool to put in your toolbox. That is why there is a whole chapter later on called 'Challenge your beliefs'.

It's important to distinguish thoughts from feelings. A thought is something that we generate between our ears. We often do this in words, e.g. 'Ellen is going to be fed up'. Sometimes we do this in images, e.g. we generate a picture of Ellen being fed up. A feeling, by contrast, is an emotional or physical sensation. We can feel this in different parts of our body, or overall. Thoughts are usually phrases or sentences. Feelings can be described in single words, e.g. anger, fear, joy, embarrassment, guilt, sadness. It is the feelings that really have an effect on us, but they are triggered off by thoughts.

DO IT!

Pick someone you know well. Let them enter your thoughts. Now dwell hard on a negative thought about them – something you believe or remember. Take a few deep breaths. Now dwell hard on a positive thought about them – something you believe or remember. Note down the thoughts and how they make you feel:

negative thought: _____

feeling: _____

positive thought: _____

feeling: _____

What do you conclude from this?

TAKING ACTION

It may seem obvious, but it still needs stating. Understanding what the problem is, committing yourself to change, recording your thinking and other data – all these are important. But they are all for nothing if you do not take action.

To help you take action, the learning log at the end of each chapter ends with a column called 'What I can do'. The two entries on page 6, for example, could be completed like this:

DATE	WHAT HAPPENED	WHAT I LEARNED	WHAT I CAN DO
6 June	Blew up at work again	I noticed that I was really stressed before I lost it – tight chested and breathing fast. But taking a few deep breaths helped calm me down	Remember to breathe deeply when I feel agitated.
7 June	Spoke to manager about shift problem	I thought he'd be dismissive and I'd get mad. But he actually listened. Addressing the issue stopped me building up resentful feelings.	Try not to imagine people reacting badly when I say something controversial. That will help me take a risk and say what I'm feeling.

Fig. 1.9 Learning log with action points

Taking action also means practising. As an angry man, you are almost certainly in the habit of thinking and acting in particular ways. Breaking these habits will be uncomfortable, even difficult, at first. So you need to practise the new habits until they become as automatic as your old bad habits.

Often taking action consists of very small steps. Consciously noting your thinking before you 'lose it' is taking action. Challenging your thinking, even after the event, is taking action. Practising doing this over a period of a week is taking action. Bringing the challenge forward so that you turn the heat down on your anger just once is taking action. All these acts are steps that take you closer to your goal (see Fig. 1.10).

1. Consciously noting your thinking before you 'lose it'
2. Challenging your thinking after the event
3. Practising doing this over a period of a week
4. Bringing the challenge forward so that you get less angry

Fig. 1.10 How individual actions
bring you closer to your goal

Often taking action will mean experimenting. You will try things out and see what difference it makes. It is important that you see setbacks as learning experiences rather than signs of failure. There is a very wise saying which encapsulates this: 'Not Failure But Feedback'. It makes a big difference which F-word you use. Labelling steps as failures, or (even worse) yourself as a failure, demotivates you so that you stay stuck. Seeing what you can learn from apparent failures allows you to move on.

TOOLKIT

- Try hard to understand why you get angry, even if at first you think you can't do anything about it.

- Make a commitment to change.

- Get used to recording information about your anger.

- Notice what you are thinking, and how your thoughts directly result in your feelings.

- Take action and practise new habits.

- When you have a setback, learn from it. Say 'Not failure but feedback'.

learning log

WHAT I HAVE LEARNT	WHAT I CAN DO

2 | OWN UP
YOU'RE ANGRY

AIMS

- To explore whether you really are angry
- To discover what makes anger a problem
- To understand why men often deny that they are angry
- To challenge three key myths that undermine responsibility for anger
- To commit to taking responsibility for change

Why a chapter on owning up to anger? Surely if you are reading this book you have already done that?

Well, yes and no. You could have found this book in your Christmas stocking, your partner's last ditch attempt to turn your relationship round. You could be browsing in a bookshop. You could have an inkling that you have a problem and want to find out more. You could be terrified that you are in fact angry, so you need to prove to yourself that you aren't.

Besides, anger has many sides to it. How do you know if the anger you are feeling isn't justified? Is *any* anger justified? Where is the point when appropriate anger tips over into anger that needs 'management'?

Men in particular can find themselves denying that they have an anger problem. Denying they are angry has the short term consequences that they don't have to feel guilty or responsible. It's the other person's fault, isn't it? But the mid and longer term consequences are dire: the problem continues, the pain it causes continues, the guilt about not dealing with it continues, at least at some deeper unacknowledged level. All these ingredients make the situation worse. It's a classic vicious circle (see Fig. 2.1).

Fig. 2.1 The vicious circle of denial

HOW DO I KNOW IF I HAVE A PROBLEM?

We will be looking in more detail at what anger actually is in the next chapter. Here it is more helpful to start at the other end – to consider what its effects may be. Because it is only through its effects that you will truly know if you have a problem with anger.

Do you recognise yourself in any of these patterns?

Cal is hot under the collar a lot of the time. It doesn't take much to push him over the edge. What that means in practice may only be snapping at his son, or exploding with curses when he can't get the computer to work properly, or driving far too fast because he is so worked up. He is irritable and grumpy, and he notices that his family and work colleagues are keeping him more and more at a distance, treating him with kid gloves.

Norrie is happy and outgoing most of the time. In fact he can't do enough to help other people and sort things out. He has a loving family and an interesting job that fulfils him. But sometimes the red mist descends apparently out of nowhere. He 'loses it' big time, usually in an argument. This terrifies the person on the end of it – usually his wife – but it also frightens Norrie. And shames him. Losing control like this wasn't in his script, and he doesn't know what to do about it.

Rob has a happy home life but has become a demon at work. The recession has resulted in staff cut backs, and the threat of further redundancies. He is working late most nights. What is making the situation worse is that he is treating his team more and more contemptuously, putting them down, being openly rude and shouting at them when their work isn't up to scratch. With his superiors he is compliant on the outside but seething with resentment underneath.

Hussein lost his job a year ago, and has been struggling to make ends meet since then. His dreams of providing a firm foundation for his wife and young family have evaporated. He spends a lot of time brooding over what has happened to him. He drinks too much. And occasionally he goes on a rampage, wrecking the bedroom or picking a fight with someone at the pub.

These men are all very different, and their circumstances are different. The way they express their anger is different. But there is a common thread that makes each of them wonder whether they have an anger problem. This thread is that the effects of their anger are significantly negative or detrimental. This is when an expression of anger is more than just anger – it becomes a disorder.

The American Psychiatric Association has a good definition of a disorder:

> *A disorder results when an individual experiences considerable emotional distress or significant impairment in relationships with others or significant impairment as a wage earner, homemaker, or student.*

Ask yourself these questions:

- Is my anger really getting in the way of me achieving what I want to do, of being effective at work or elsewhere in my life? Is it stopping me solving problems effectively?

- Is my anger significantly affecting my relationships, with my partner, other members of my family, friends or colleagues?

- Is my anger frightening me because of its unpredictability, so that I feel out of control? Or because of its destructive power? Or because of the strain it puts on my heart?

- Is my anger in none of those categories, but it worries and annoys me because it's around so much? It's such a drag being so irritable, it can't be good for me and I feel stuck in a pattern that I simply want to change.

If your answer to any one of these questions is Yes, then you have acknowledged that you have an anger problem.

DO IT!

Write down all the different effects that you think your anger has. You could draw up a table under these headings:

RELATIONSHIPS	EFFECTIVENESS	FEELINGS	HEALTH

ASSESS YOURSELF

Sometimes it helps to have an objective measure to assess whether you have a problem. Here is an activity that may help you do that. Each of the situations listed may provoke an angry response. Of course this often depends on the circumstances, so you have to generalise. But put yourself in the situation and imagine how angry you would feel as a general rule. Rate your anger on the following scale:

1 – VERY LITTLE   4 – MUCH

2 – LITTLE   5 – VERY MUCH

3 – A MODERATE AMOUNT

1. You unpack an appliance you have just bought, plug it in, and discover that it doesn't work

2. Being overcharged by a repair person who has you over a barrel

3. Being singled out for a correction, while the actions of others go unnoticed

4. Getting your car stuck in the mud or sand

5. You are talking to someone and they don't answer you

6. Someone pretends to be something they are not

7. While you are struggling to carry four cups of coffee to your table at a cafeteria, someone bumps into you, spilling the coffee

8. You have hung up your clothes, but someone knocks them to the floor and fails to pick them up

9. You are hounded by a sales person from the moment you walk into the store

10. You have made arrangements to go somewhere with a person who backs off at the last minute and leaves you dangling

11. Being joked about or teased

12. Your car is stalled at a traffic light, and the person behind you keeps blowing his horn

13. You accidentally make the wrong kind of turn in a car park. As you get out of your car someone yells at you, "where did you learn to drive?"

14. Someone makes a mistake and blames it on you

15. You are trying to concentrate, but a person near you is tapping their foot

16. You lend someone an important book or tool, and they fail to return it

17. You have had a busy day, and the person you live with starts to complain about how you forgot to do something you agreed to

18. You are trying to discuss something important with your mate or partner who isn't giving you a chance to express your feelings

19. You are in a discussion with someone who persists in arguing about a topic they know very little about

20. Someone sticks his or her nose into an argument between you and someone else

21. You need to get somewhere quickly, but the car in front of you is going 40 mph in a 60 mph zone, and you can't pass

22. Stepping on a lump of chewing gum

23. Being mocked by a small group of people as you pass them

24. In a hurry to get somewhere, you tear a good pair of trousers on a sharp object

25. You reach the shopping cart page while buying something online, and just when you have filled in all your details you lose internet connection

Add up your scores. If you have given yourself 70 or below it is unlikely that you have a problem with anger. Between 70 and 85 your problem is moderate but you definitely need to work on it. If your score is over 85 then your problem is severe and requires urgent attention.

One caveat: you will have noted Norrie's case above. He may not have scored highly in this test, because the number of times he explodes with anger are few and far between. But the effect these explosions has on him and his partner are huge. For Norrie, his anger is a problem. You may be like Norrie.

TAKING RESPONSIBILITY

We began this chapter by explaining how men often deny that they are angry. This denial can take several forms. The subtlest forms are those when we recognise that we are angry, but we don't take responsibility for it. The following three statements are the commonest examples that I hear in my consulting room:

- 'I'm not in control of myself when I'm angry.'
- 'I can't do anything about it – I've always been angry.'
- 'It's x and y that make me angry.'

Let's take these three statements one at a time and examine them.

1 *'I'm not in control of myself when I'm angry.'*

It certainly feels that way, doesn't it? The red mist descends and you behave in a way that afterwards shocks and shames you. It feels as if you were on a conveyer belt of actions and feelings and that you couldn't get off until the end of the journey.

But as we will see in chapter 4, even when you are in the heart of the tempest, there are things you can do to take more control. (Note: not gain complete control but take more control.) And there are certainly lots of things that you can do in advance to ensure that your response, when provoked, is more managed and less destructive.

So saying that you are not in control is at best a half-truth, and at worst a cop out.

2 *'I can't do anything about it – I've always been angry.'*

This is another statement based on despair. The idea is that if you have always been something you always will be. It's illogical, isn't it?

It's also very stuck. The image is of a stagnant pool of water, never changing but getting more and more revolting. How helpful is that? Instead, think of your life as a flowing river, carving its way across rough ground, alive and dynamic.

Certainly your anger may be the habit of a lifetime. But you will be delighted to hear that however long the habit, it can take a matter of weeks to break. It takes a bit of time, therefore, and some effort. Only you can decide whether that effort is worth it.

DO IT!

Think of a time when you put time and effort into something – a task, a relationship, a skill, whatever. (And by 'time' I mean active time – not just 'suffering' something for a period. That's passive time.) What was the result?

On the whole, do you get results when you apply time and effort to something?

Think of any habits that you have changed. How did you do this? Now decide whether you want to make changes to your anger.

So 'I've always been like it' is no reason to continue like it.

3 'It's x and y that make me angry.'

It's very easy, and very common, to say that it's your wife who made you angry, or the shop assistant, or the faulty printer. But it's completely wrong.

Remember our businessmen on the train? (See page 10 above.) If the young men were able to make Sacha extremely angry AND Paul amused AND Alan mildly annoyed AND Ashwani full of goodwill AND Peter inadequate and regretful AND Alex anxious, then they were hugely powerful young men!

If another passenger had become so distressed at their laughing and joking that he had shot everyone in the carriage, would the young men have been responsible for that too?

No – each person is 100% responsible for their own reactions. The young men were merely the trigger. That trigger can be provocative – in some cases hugely provocative – but we are all responsible for how we choose to react to that trigger.

Men often shy away from taking responsibility because it feels like that's the same as being blamed. Blame means criticism, and men are not quick to open themselves to criticism. But taking responsibility is very different from taking blame. Blame is backward looking, judgemental and static. Responsibility is forward looking, active and empowering (see Fig. 2.2).

BLAME / RESPONSIBILITY

Fig. 2.2 The difference between blame and responsibility

So taking responsibility is actually good news. It means:

- Other people cannot control my feelings and actions
- I can (with a bit of effort) choose to act differently
- It is in my power to make positive changes in my life

DO IT!

Write: I am responsible for how I react.

That means I choose to ....[complete]

It also means it is in my power to ....[complete]

copymaster 9

COMMITTING TO CHANGE

In chapter 1 I talked about the key skill of commitment. Making a promise to yourself to change a pattern of behaviour means these two things:

- A commitment to take responsibility for what is yours – that you are part of the problem
- A commitment to take effective action to turn the situation round – that you are part of the solution.

How can you make these commitments and maintain them? Nobody likes being reminded that we have a problem and that we need to do something about it. It's easier to avoid the issue, or pretend it doesn't happen, or blame someone else.

But you know that's what you have been doing up to now. And where has it got you?

It's more effective to take responsibility and focus on the benefits of commitment.

To help you think about what you want to change and what skills and resources you could bring to bear, draw up a statement like the one in Fig. 2.3 and fill it in. Note that it includes thinking about possible roadblocks on the route to change. The aim is to be realistic and prepared.

copymaster 10

MANAGING ANGER AND IRRITATION   27   **FIX IT** Toolkits for men © Kim Richardson 2010

1. What precisely is your goal with relation to anger?

2. What would your life be like if this goal is achieved?

3. What personal strengths can you draw on to help you achieve this goal?

4. What blocks might get in the way of you achieving this goal?

5. Do you accept responsibility for bringing about these changes in your life?

6. My commitment to change is contained in the following statement:

Signature: Date:

Fig. 2.3 Example of a statement of commitment

TOOLKIT

- Do an audit of the effects of your anger to assess how big a problem it is.

- Use an objective measure of anger, such as ones published here or on the internet, to gauge your anger.

- Get real. Take responsibility for your anger – that means empowering you to make changes.

- Write a statement of commitment to change.

learning log

WHAT I HAVE LEARNT	WHAT I CAN DO

3 | UNDERSTAND YOUR ANGER

AIMS

- To understand what anger actually is, and the different parts of the anger process
- To uncover the patterns in your own anger, including what triggers it
- To understand the four main factors that keep you spinning round the angry cycle
- To explore the effects of suppressing or expressing anger

ANGER IS A FEELING

It's important to begin with this statement: Anger is a feeling.

Anger is actually a very basic human feeling. It often occurs when we feel under attack in some way. Our primitive response to attack is to defend ourselves. That means preparing our body to fight back, or to run away. Either way, when you feel anger, chemicals including adrenalin are released into your bloodstream. Your heart rate increases. Your energy levels soar. You will think in extreme ways rather than rational, carefully considered ways. You will be full of tension and ready to react instantly.

All of these reactions have helped us to defend ourselves in our distant past, when life really was full of danger, and the possibility of attack lay round every corner. Anger is the feeling that allows us to choose 'fight' from the 'flight or fight' options.

But 'fight' does not necessarily mean physical aggression - it means responding to a perceived wrong. So we must not confuse anger with aggression. Anger is an emotion; aggression is a behaviour. We can feel angry without being violent. Men, however, are more likely than women to display aggression when they are angry.

Feelings are feelings – they are neither good nor bad. They are what you feel. They are a sign that something important is going on. Often an angry feeling is actually helpful, as it can inspire you to take effective action to tackle an injustice, or to rise above a frustration.

DO
IT !

Do not automatically judge anger. Think about times when you have been angry and it has actually (genuinely) helped you achieve something positive. What level of anger did you feel? How did you express that anger?

But all too often angry feelings can have negative effects. When we continue to display the same 'fight or flight' reaction today, even though it is usually not a life or death situation, we can get ourselves and others into trouble:

- Our relationships suffer
- We feel bad about ourselves, so our self-esteem suffers
- We are less effective in sorting situations out – usually we make them worse
- Our health suffers: increased blood pressure, gastrointestinal problems, heart attacks, strokes and a damaged immune system.
- We (especially men) are more likely to turn to aggression.

If you can't decide whether the anger that you are feeling and expressing is positive or not, go back to basics. Do an audit of the effect that it is having. Think about each of the bullet points above in turn. Ask yourself – is the anger proportionate to the offence? Is it effective in the short and long term? (See chapter 2 on making an anger audit.)

MANAGING ANGER

How you got to that place of anger, and what you are going to do with it while you are there, are separate things. Even 'how you got there' consists of at least two things – the trigger for your anger and the thoughts and assumptions you bring to the situation.

The process is described in Fig. 3.1.

TRIGGER --> THOUGHTS/ASSUMPTIONS --> ANGRY FEELING --> EXPRESSION

Fig. 3.1 The process of anger

So when we talk about anger management, we can mean any of the following:

- Managing the triggers that set off the process
- Managing your thoughts and assumptions to reduce the angry feelings
- Managing the level of your anger once you are angry
- Managing the way you express your anger once you get angry.

This book helps you manage the process at each of these key points (see Fig. 3.2).

TRIGGER --> THOUGHTS/ASSUMPTIONS --> ANGRY FEELING --> EXPRESSION

| Managing triggers can be helpful, but it often is not possible. Because triggers are things that usually happen to you. We will be looking further at triggers below, and how to manage them in chapter 4. | Managing your thoughts and assumptions is extremely helpful – we will focus on this in chapter 5, but refer to it throughout the book. | Managing the level of your anger is very helpful as long as your anger is at a low enough level for you to think rationally. See chapter 8. Once you are ready to explode with anger, there is less you can do (but see chapter 4 for the emergency toolkit). | Managing the way you express your anger also can be helpful. We look at assertiveness in chapter 8. However, men who get really angry are often past the stage of being able to express it effectively. By then it is too late. |

Fig. 3.2 Managing the
process of anger

TRIGGERS

There are two main types of thing that can trigger an angry reaction:

- Irritants
- Loss, or threat of loss.

Irritants are things that irritate us. Things that wind us up. Tools being borrowed and not returned. Or not returned in the right place. People who speak too loudly. People who speak too softly. Phone lines that break up. Slow drivers. Bad drivers.

The list is potentially endless. Each one of us will have his own personal list. What irritates one man will not necessarily irritate another. (That is because people think about things differently – see chapter 5.)

How do irritants relate to the fight or flight response described earlier? Sometimes the irritant feels like an attack in itself. Your teenager's music played at full blast. The coin that 'deliberately' gets rejected by the car park machine.

Sometimes the attack is more subtle. You have an unwritten rule that people shouldn't drive under 25 mph in a 30 mph area. When they break that rule you feel affronted. Why can't everyone follow your sensible rules? When your rules are broken, you feel diminished, at risk.

The second category of triggers relate to loss. This may means loss of time, such as losing some work on the computer (which you will then have to redo). Or loss of money, such as your partner scraping the car.

But for men the biggest loss is the loss of face. Something is happening which either means you are losing face, or there is a danger that will happen. You will be laughed at. Or judged. Criticised. This kind of loss can be triggered by all sorts of things - being interrupted, or a criticism that you are not bringing in enough income. Or that you can't fix the car.

It doesn't take much to see how this kind of trigger can appear like a savage attack on our status, one that must be defended at all costs.

Read back over the last seven paragraphs. What kind of belief or assumption (rule) would someone have to have to respond angrily to each trigger? For example:

TRIGGERS	BELIEFS / ASSUMPTIONS
Tool being borrowed and not returned	'My tool has not been returned - this is irritating!' [thought] 'When things are borrowed they must be returned' [assumption/rule]

This activity will help you see that it isn't the trigger that makes you angry – it's your beliefs about the event. More on this in chapter 5.

My clients are often unclear about what triggers their anger. 'It just comes out of the blue.' 'It could be anything.' But this lack of clarity contributes to the problem. Because we hate being unclear, taken by surprise, baffled. It disempowers us.

So it is important as a first step in getting more control over our anger that we are aware of the triggers. That means spending a bit of time gathering the data.

Draw up an anger diary for a week. It can be very simple, like the one below. The trigger is the event or situation that resulted in you being angry. If you can rate your anger each time on a scale of 1 to 10, that will help. When you look back over your diary you will be able to see what things trigger your anger and how much.

DATE	TRIGGER	FEELING
3 June	Rachel accuses me of being lazy	Furious, upset 7/10

You may want to keep this going for longer than a week. The more patterns you notice, the more helpful this exercise is.

We will look further at what you can do about triggers in chapter 4.

CYCLES OF ANGER

Some clients say to me, 'If getting angry gets me into such trouble, why do I do it?' It's a good question. Answering it helps us to understand anger a bit more, which again is another step on the road to dealing with it.

There are four main reasons why we continue to get angry in a destructive way. Usually at least two of these factors are at work at the same time:

- Temperament
- The influence of key experiences and role models
- The force of habit
- Short-term 'benefits'.

1 *Temperament.*

We can deal with this very quickly, simply by saying there is nothing we can do about it! If we are born with the 'quick to anger' gene, then we have to accept that. Note – this does not mean we can excuse ourselves. Accepting ourselves also means taking responsibility for ourselves. In this case, we have to work even harder at the trickier aspects of the hand that fate has dealt us.

2 *The influence of key experiences and role models.*

Our early experiences have a huge impact on how we view ourselves and the world. These 'core beliefs' will in turn lead to us act in particular ways, and make certain assumptions. As we will see later, we can adapt our core beliefs and assumptions, however deeply they are rooted in experience.

Many angry men have angry fathers. Or mothers. They may have had other angry role models at key points in their lives. Many were brought up without the means of dealing with anger effectively. Our role models are important factors, but again we cannot usually change them. The best we can do is to notice the effect they have had, and decide to act differently.

Dan was brought up by a highly critical mother and distant father; his father left the family home when he was a teenager. Dan's mother would regularly reduce him to tears with her savage angry attacks. His brother seemed to escape her wrath. Filled with injustice, Dan grew up to see the world as a dangerous place, expecting attack and blame, and alternately turning his anger on himself and others when things went wrong. Being bullied at secondary school reinforced his view of the world.

DO IT!

Think about angry people who have had a big influence on your life. What is the behaviour that you 'learnt' from them?

It could be that anger was not allowed or expressed where you were brought up. What, then, did you learn about anger in that case?

Think about any key experiences or critical incidents in your life which you associate with being angry now. When and how were you the victim of attack or injustice?

3 *Habit.*

Habits are very powerful, mainly because they reinforce themselves. The more you do something, the more likely it is that you will repeat it. The brain notices a pattern – certain situations, thoughts, feelings and reactions all coming together – and 'pattern matches' similar situations. The advantage is that we don't have to process every separate situation as if it is totally new. The disadvantage is that it reduces the variety of our responses.

We can get into the habit of anger, just as others can get into the habit of depression, or guilt, or generosity. The good news is that even habits of a lifetime can be unlearned remarkably quickly.

4 *Short-term 'benefits'.*

The most powerful reason why we can continue in a habit that is self-destructive is because we actually do feel some benefits from it, at least in the short term. These are:

- It is an easy response, because we are used to it (see 'habit' above).
- When we feel threatened, our body is primed to attack. Being angry actually releases some of this pressure, and can therefore be physically pleasurable.
- We avoid the real issue, which appears to be even worse than being angry. This may be acknowledging a more difficult feeling, or facing our fears and being assertive.

We will have more to say about the last 'benefit' in chapter 5. For the present, it is enough to say that all of these benefits are, of course, not really to our advantage. Because in the mid to long term they make us feel much worse. The simple fact is that the effects of destructive anger, whether short term or long term, all contribute to the cycle being repeated (see Fig. 3.3).

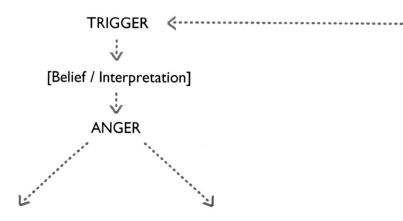

TRIGGER

↓

[Belief / Interpretation]

↓

ANGER

SHORT-TERM POSITIVES:

• it's easy
• release of pressure
• avoids more difficult issue

MID/LONG-TERM NEGATIVES:

• health damage
• self and others feel worse
• doesn't solve problems
• confirms image and habit as angry man

CONSEQUENCE

more likely to respond
angrily again

Fig. 3.3 The cycle of anger

Draw up a cost-benefit analysis of the effects of keeping your angry habit going. Two simple columns: Advantages and Disadvantages.

Now return to the things you put in the 'Advantages' column. Should any of these go in the other column as well?

Looking at your analysis overall, what conclusions do you come to?

copymaster 19

PATTERNS OF ANGER

Recognising our own pattern of anger can also help us take control. In my experience men fall into one of four patterns:

- The long-burning fuse
- The domino effect
- The stew
- The Roman candle.

1 The *long-burning* fuse is the 'out of the blue' explosion. A single incident, or remark, is apparently enough to provoke a furious reaction or argument. The explosion is all the more shocking because it is unexpected. That's because the fuse is hidden, and it gets eaten up by the flame quietly.

2 A *domino effect* occurs when there are a series of small angry outbursts. Each one adds fuel to the next, until there is the 'final straw' when they ignite a major explosion.

3 The *stew* is a common pattern in men who suppress their anger. They don't have the means to express it safely (or so they think). So they stew on the angry thoughts instead. Eventually the stew boils over.

4 The *Roman candle* burns gently a lot of the time, but is always in danger of firing out sparks. It sputters and fizzles, overreacting here, making savage put-downs there. The candle can keep burning for a long time like this.

THE LONG-BURNING FUSE

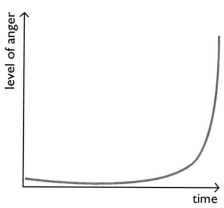

THE DOMINO EFFECT

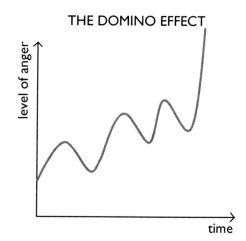

THE STEW

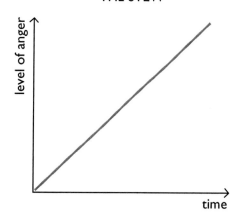

THE ROMAN CANDLE

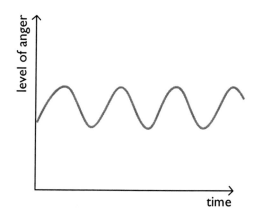

Fig. 3.4 Four patterns of anger

Think about your own pattern of anger. Does it fit with any of the patterns described here? Or is it a combination of patterns?

What can you learn about the fact that you may react in a particular pattern?

42 **FIX IT** Toolkits for men © Kim Richardson 2010

Rob realised that his pattern was to stew. He would take his partner Susie's comments to heart and dwell on them, sometimes all evening and into the night. Then, in the morning it wouldn't take much to tip him over the edge. Once, when Susie had gone to work, he destroyed the kitchen.

Recognising this pattern led him to think more closely about the stewing period. He realised that he had to speak up and deal with things more openly when they happened. That was uncomfortable, but facing this fear was better than continuing to feel bad, then explode.

SUPPRESS IT OR EXPRESS IT?

Suppressing anger means keeping it in, keeping the lid on it at all costs. Some men have been taught that this is what you do with anger. The underlying message might be, 'Anger is wrong' or 'If I show anger something bad will happen.'

However, suppressing anger is usually harmful and ineffective. Look back at the 'stewing' graph in Fig. 3.4. Men who suppress generally end up exploding. If they don't explode outwards, they can explode inwards, damaging themselves through depression or self-harm.

If you catch yourself thinking, 'Anger is wrong', remind yourself that anger is a feeling. Feelings are not right or wrong, they just are. *Expressing* anger in particular ways could be 'wrong', but that's a different matter.

Expressing anger means addressing the feeling and doing something about it. That may involve stating your concerns, showing your annoyance in a constructive, assertive way. It may mean letting off steam in a controlled 'safe' way such as punching cushions or going for a run.

Expressing anger is NOT the same thing as 'letting it all out' or boiling over. That happens when you have let the situation develop too long, or when you are no longer in control. Healthy expression of anger happens at an earlier stage. These are the benefits of expressing angry feelings at an early stage, in an appropriate way:

- It defuses tension before it reaches dangerous levels
- It allows you to communicate what you want
- It helps your self-esteem and your relationships
- It is better for your physical health.

TURNING THE HEAT DOWN

'Suppression or expression' as actually one of those 'false choices' that we often present ourselves with. The overall aim in anger management is not to suppress or to express, but to TURN THE HEAT DOWN. This can be achieved in many ways, only one of which is actually expressing the angry feelings (see Fig. 3.5)

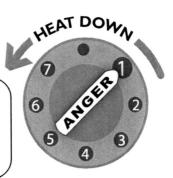

What turns the heat of anger down

- Express appropriately
- Let off steam safely
- Challenge beliefs – turn anger to annoyance
- Deal with the real issues – self-esteem, depression, stress
- Take emergency measures

What turns the heat of anger up

- Suppress
- Express angrily and aggressively
- Explode

Fig. 3.5 Turning the heat
of anger down or up

Later on you will be exploring in more detail the different methods of turning the heat down on your anger.

The thermostat is a useful image for many men. Having a picture of what creates a problem, and how to deal with it, can help us get a handle on it. If the thermostat doesn't work for you, try a different image, such as the leaky tank.

We can store angry feelings inside us, like liquid in a tank. Unless these are dealt with effectively, they rise … and rise … and then overflow (see Fig. 3.6).

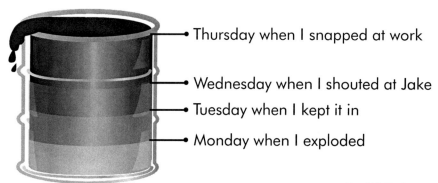

Thursday when I snapped at work

Wednesday when I shouted at Jake

Tuesday when I kept it in

Monday when I exploded

Fig. 3.6 Storing up anger in a tank

How do we stop the liquid constantly overflowing? We can punch holes in the tank so that it leaks away into the ground harmlessly. Each of the tools already mentioned is effectively a hole that you punch into your tank of anger (see Fig. 3.7).

copymaster 23

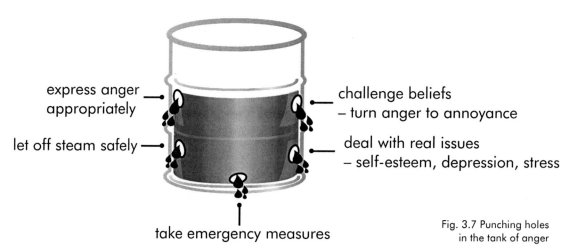

express anger appropriately

let off steam safely

challenge beliefs – turn anger to annoyance

deal with real issues – self-esteem, depression, stress

take emergency measures

Fig. 3.7 Punching holes in the tank of anger

DO IT!

Think about whether you are guilty of suppressing anger, or of 'letting it all out'. Or maybe a mixture of the two?

Choose one of the images of anger – a heating system or an overflowing tank – and commit to turning the heat down, or letting your anger leak away.

TOOLKIT

• Allow yourself to feel anger – and express it – when it is genuinely helpful to do so. Remember that anger itself is not bad. The way you express it may be.

• Understand that the anger process includes triggers, thoughts, feelings and action. Tell yourself that you can intervene at any of these stages to make a difference.

• Get to know your own pattern of anger, including what triggers it. Gather the data as a first step towards making changes.

• Question whether the 'benefits' of letting off steam in an explosive way really are benefits.

• Imagine your anger as a heating system or an overflowing tank. Commit to turning the heat down, or letting your anger leak away.

learning log

WHAT I HAVE LEARNT	WHAT I CAN DO

4 | TAKE CONTROL

AIMS

- To give you some emergency tools to prevent you tipping over from anger into rage or violence.
- To explore how talking to someone or throwing yourself into a different activity can help you let off steam.
- To find ways of avoiding things that trigger your anger.
- To discuss the role of drink and drugs in the cycle of anger.

EMERGENCY TOOLS

This chapter begins with your emergency toolkit. It is intended to give you the tools to prevent you tipping over from anger into rage or violence. To control yourself so that you can come back from the brink of spoiling your life or someone else's. (Usually both.)

It is a short section, for two reasons.

- Emergency tools need to be quick and easy to use.
- Emergency tools are effectively just sticking plaster. The real work you have to do is to tackle the underlying causes of your anger.

Remember that there are degrees of anger (see Fig. 4.1).

ANNOYANCE --> ANGER --> RAGE --> VIOLENCE

Fig. 4.1 The spectrum of anger

What we are talking about here is how to restrain yourself from moving beyond anger into rage. Rage is when your anger is out of control. You have 'lost it'. It is a tiny step from this to physical violence.

CASE STUDY

Paul has had enough of the demands put upon him by his wife, Ruth. He seems to be working longer and longer hours for less and less income, but Ruth seems to be nagging at him to do more. He has tried to shrug this off until one evening when a critical comment from Ruth is like a spark falling on dry leaves. Paul screams at her, his face contorted, his fists clenched. Afterwards he was told he ranted for several minutes, but he could remember very little of it. He could remember striking Ruth, though, and the fear and guilt that followed.

When we are enraged, like Paul, we are in danger of doing serious damage. Physical damage as well as emotional damage, because we are even less in control of our reactions than when we are just angry. We say and do things that afterwards often we can hardly believe.

One way of explaining this is to see it as an extreme version of the 'flight or fight' stress response. Adrenalin surges through us. We don't think rationally – we hardly think at all. We feel under attack and we react with supercharged aggression.

Afterwards, when we have calmed down, we may be so shocked that we deny or make light of what has happened. Or we blame it on someone or something else. But the simple fact is that however out of control you may feel, you are still 100% responsible for your reactions.

Violence is always unjustified. It is also usually against the law. Often it is directed at women or children, who are often less able to defend themselves. Stopping yourself from becoming violent is essential.

If you think you have no choice but to respond with rage and violence when you are provoked, consider this: If the person you last raged at or thought of hitting was a 2 metre tall policeman, would you really have gone ahead?
No, you would have chosen to hold back. However out of control you feel, there is always an element of choice in your reaction.

Violence against objects can also be dangerous and shocking. It can be 'directed at' another so that the partner whose favourite object is destroyed is both upset at the damage and fearful that it may be them next. Violence against objects can also be violence against the self. Plunging a fist through glass is partly a form of self-harm.

So what emergency tools are available for those who want to pull back from the brink? I can offer three:

- Counting to ten
- Removing yourself from the scene
- Breathing

1 *Counting to ten* is simply a way of giving yourself a chance to calm down, to bring the dial down from rage or violence to anger or even annoyance. Ten seconds may not seem like a very long time, but it can be enough to save a situation from irreparable harm. When you are counting, remember to focus on the numbers one … two … three … in your head. This is an additional means of distraction which will help you take the heat out of your anger.

2 *Removing yourself from the scene* is also very simple. You may *feel* cornered, but it is rare that you are physically unable to take yourself away. Moving away allows you to calm down as it is another form of distraction. Say, 'I need to take five here,' and go into another room. Or if you feel provoked in public, just turn and walk away.

It is important that when you remove yourself from the scene you work at calming yourself down (for example by breathing slowly and giving yourself helpful messages). Walking away and brooding will only make your anger worse.

If your rage or violence is directed at your partner, it helps to have an agreement with her (or him) that taking time out means you are trying to regain control. It is not a sign of weakness. Pursuing you usually makes the situation worse; instead, ask if they can agree to wait and let you return when you are more in control of your anger.

3 _Breathing_ is an extremely effective way of turning the heat down on your anger. When we go into fight or flight mode, we start breathing in a very shallow way, or even stop breathing altogether, in preparation for action. Reversing this process has immediate physiological effects. A few deep breaths from the belly (not from the chest) will give powerful messages to the brain that you are calming down, and so will actually calm you down. See Fig. 4.2. (We will have more to say about breathing in chapter 9.)

PRACTISE SLOW BREATHING:

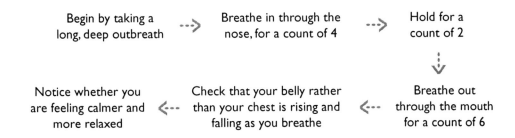

Fig. 4.2 Breathing to reduce arousal

DO IT!

When you are in danger of tipping over from anger to rage or violence, the anger habit kicks in very strongly. So you need something powerful to counteract it.

You will need to commit yourself in advance to using one of these three emergency tools. Write:

When I am angry, I commit myself to …..........…….. to prevent myself from raging or getting violent.

I recognise that rage and violence does no good, and a lot of harm.

Getting someone to witness your commitment is also very helpful. Then put your commitment into practice.

LETTING OFF STEAM

A second layer of emergency tools comes under the heading of 'letting off steam'.

We have to be careful here, for two reasons. First, letting off steam is often not the best way of getting rid of angry feelings. We discussed this in chapter 3. Exploding angrily is more likely to make you angrier. If you act angry you will feel angry.

Second, it never deals with the root cause of your anger in the first place.

Letting off steam at the person who has provoked your anger in the first place may at times appear to give you what you want. For example, it may release some of the tension that has been building up in you. Or even release chemicals that make you enjoy the experience of exploding. It may also frighten your tormentor, so that you 'get what you want' or can feel powerful or superior.

But you know that all these effects are extremely short-term. In the mid and long term the damage done far outweighs these little 'victories' (see Fig. 4.3).

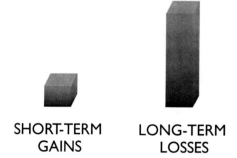

SHORT-TERM
GAINS

LONG-TERM
LOSSES

Fig. 4.3 The gains and losses of expressing anger

Viewed from this perspective, these victories look more like defeats.

So I recommend letting off steam only under these conditions:

- You do it in a controlled way (as in the examples below) and not at anyone.
- You do it to turn the heat down from rage/violence to ordinary anger, not as a way of tackling what makes you angry in the first place. It is an emergency tool, not a solution.

If you find yourself in a familiar situation of being on the brink, you could let off steam by doing two things – talking to someone or distracting into an activity.

1 *Talking to someone* you trust can help you get things off your chest. It is also a way of getting a bit of distance from the issue. Often by talking we see things in a different way. That is especially the case if the person you are talking to can gently challenge you. Beware of sharing your angry feelings with someone who will simply goad you on – this will do you no favours at all.

<table>
<tr>
<td>CASE STUDY</td>
<td>Tom was brewing up for a fight. His neighbour had parked too close to his driveway three times in the last fortnight, and now he had done it again. Already smarting from a difficult meeting with his boss, Tom felt his anger swell to rage. He had visions of him storming next door and 'punching his lights out'. His heart was racing and his blood was boiling.

Recognising these signs he decided to park the car and rant about his neighbour to his wife. After ten minutes he had calmed down enough to realise that attacking his neighbour would be the worst choice of action. She also pointed out that they had never actually raised the issue with him. They decided to do this together.</td>
</tr>
</table>

2 *Distraction* is another good option. Choose to do anything rather than take yourself over the edge. Go for a run. Play music. Dig in the garden. Lay the new patio. As you do these things, focus on what you are doing rather than brew on your anger. Make sure you wind down after any period of vigorous activity.

As we described in chapter 3, anger is like a leaky tank. So if you let enough time pass, the angry feelings will leak away. Maybe not entirely – but enough to save you from falling into the cycle of rage and violence yet again.

Many distractions do more than just give your anger time to cool off. They also provide you with the means to feel better about yourself, physically or emotionally. We will have more to say about this in chapter 9.

DO IT!

Practise these techniques of letting off steam when you are only slightly angry. Then they will come more naturally to you when you really are on the brink. Choose a week when you commit to talking or distracting instead of openly getting angry about any situation that occurs, whether at work or at home. Consciously take these steps, and notice what happens to the heat in your anger.

Reward yourself for taking control. You will be programming yourself to act in this way when the situation is tougher, and when the stakes are higher.

If you think that distraction or taking emergency steps to draw back from violent action are not 'manly', think again. Getting enraged or violent means you are out of control. How 'manly' is that? Think of the men you admire. How many of them act out of control?

Taking charge, getting on top of things, and taking effective action – these are usually the qualities associated with 'real' men. By using these tools you will be joining them.

AVOIDING TRIGGERS

We have already spoken a lot about triggers to anger. In chapter 3 you made a trigger diary, as a way of understanding what things sparked you off.

One way in which you can use this sort of information is to get wise before the event. If you truly are committed to taking control, then you will want to avoid flashpoints and other situations that may trigger your angry response.

You can avoid in different ways. Sometimes it is enough literally to avoid the person or thing that regularly triggers your anger. If there is a particular person at work who drives you crazy, it makes sense not to engage with that person whenever possible. If there is a bottleneck at a particular junction on your way to work which always leaves you ready for a fight from 8.30 in the morning, then go a different way, or leave at a different time to avoid it.

Sometimes avoiding a trigger means you need to be a bit more creative. Your partner always forgets to put the rubbish out, and that is like a red rag to a bull when you come home on a Friday. So put it out yourself.

You could say, 'Why should I, it's her job and I do everything else.' But where does that get you? You both lose out, because you get mad and she bears the brunt of your anger. Think creatively – maybe you can swap jobs.

Remember that you can't change other people, but you can change yourself. In situations like the one described above, take credit for taking control rather than hanging on to a resentment that continues to fester and do damage.

Avoiding triggers is often a short-term solution. If the person at work who you constantly avoid for fear of getting into a rage is your boss, or a close colleague, then clearly you need to address what the problem really is. You cannot continue to avoid them indefinitely!

One way of avoiding triggers that is *not* to be recommended is using drugs or alcohol. Recreational drugs may relax you, but they can contribute to your anger problem. This is because they reduce your ability to deal with the ordinary challenges of life – let alone its crises. Often men are angry for this very reason.

Alcohol is even more dangerous for an angry man. Its immediate effect is to relax the drinker, but it also lowers inhibitions. This means that the usual barriers that we put up to our own destructive impulses break down. Men with drink inside them are more, not less, likely to turn anger into rage, as the crime statistics so graphically show.

And the same applies to alcohol and drugs as to other avoidance strategies – they don't give you a chance to deal with the real issues that are making you angry.

If you have a problem with alcohol or drug dependency, get help.

copymaster 29

DO IT!

Look at the list of triggers that you recorded in your diary (chapter 4). Think how you could avoid each trigger by arranging your life differently. If you catch yourself saying, 'I don't see why I should do that,' consider answering by saying, 'Because it will prevent me from getting really angry, and that is my number one priority!'

CASE STUDY

Greg is an angry man for lots of reasons, but what often tips him over into bouts of rage is returning from work to a house full of noise and crying children and a stressed partner who needs him to take charge. He realises that his blood sugar level is low, and this contributes to his patience being wafer thin. He decides to experiment by having a snack while travelling home, and by reading the paper rather than working on the train. This gives him the extra energy that he needs to cope with the 7 o'clock handover.

TOOLKIT

- In an emergency, count to ten, remove yourself from the scene, and/or breathe deeply.
- Remember that you always have a choice, even if it feels as if you do not.
- Let off steam by talking to someone or throwing yourself into a different activity.
- Avoid triggers where you can. You may have to think creatively to do this.
- If you are angry, avoid drink and drugs.

learning log

WHAT I HAVE LEARNT	WHAT I CAN DO

5 | CHALLENGE YOUR BELIEFS

AIMS

- To explain how thinking errors are a major cause of men getting angry
- To identify common thinking errors that contribute to anger
- To learn how we can check out, challenge and change our thoughts
- To question the unwritten rules that men often have
- To explore how you can use imagery to reduce your anger

CHECK OUT YOUR THINKING

In chapter 1 we talked about the key role that our thoughts play in making us angry men. Remember the formula?

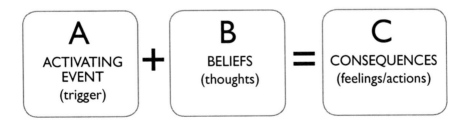

Fig. 5.1 The A B C formula

The 'C' that we are focusing on is angry feelings and angry behaviour. That's what you want to get on top of. The 'A' are the triggers that you have already identified (see page 36 above).

As we have seen, there is a limited amount of control that we have over triggers. It is difficult to prevent your partner yelling at you, your son from leaving your tools out in the rain, your neighbour from having a wild party. These things happen. It's how you *deal* with them that counts. And one of the major ways in which we deal with triggers is to think about them in particular ways.

Human beings (not just men!) get into the habit of thinking in unhelpful and unrealistic ways. Psychologists have given labels to some of these thinking errors. The labels help us to notice the errors, which is the first step towards changing the habits.

Read the list of some common thinking errors that angry men find themselves repeating (Fig. 5.2).

1) Identify which ones you use. Note their effect. They are a key reason why you get so angry.
2) Make a commitment to start turning this kind of self-defeating thinking around.
3) Read on to see how you can do this.

NAME	DESCRIPTION	EFFECT
BLACK AND WHITE THINKING	'All or nothing' thinking – we think of people, events or situations in extremes, e.g. 'I must get it absolutely right', 'She's completely in control and I am powerless'. There are no shades of grey.	Extreme thinking leads to extreme feelings. These are usually extreme negative feelings. E.g. if we think we are powerless, we will be hugely frustrated and despairing. Ideal conditions for lashing out in anger.
CATASTROPHISING	When we expect disaster, such as 'If I complain, I'll lose my job' or 'If she disagrees it will ruin the weekend.' Events and their significance are blown out of all proportion in a negative way.	Imagining and expecting the worst makes us feel very anxious and stressed, which again can easily lead to anger.
PERSONALISING	Taking things personally. Blaming ourselves unfairly or imagining that other people's actions are reactions to us, e.g. if someone is in a bad mood it's because we have upset them, or if they say 'We're starting late' they mean 'You're late.'	We become unnecessarily defensive and sensitive around other people. One result is retaliating or attacking back. We also develop a negative self-image, which we feel we have to defend all the time.
BLAMING	The opposite of personalisation – when we hold other people, organisations or even 'life' responsible for our problems, e.g. 'They made me feel terrible', 'You should have listened to me carefully.'	Always seeing the fault in others means that we never take responsibility for our own issues. We feel resentful and disempowered – an angry victim.
MIND READING	Imagining that we know what people are thinking about us and feeling towards us, e.g. 'He thinks I'm stupid', or 'She thinks I can't be trusted.'	When we mind read we usually imagine the worst, which contributes to anxious or angry feelings.
LABELLING	Putting a (negative) global label on others rather than rating their skills in a specific situation, e.g. 'He's a complete idiot.' Also labelling ourselves in a global negative way, e.g. 'I'm useless'.	Labelling others prevents us from seeing good things about them, and therefore contributes to our anger towards them. Labelling our self is hugely damaging to our self-image.
MUST-ITIS	Holding rigid beliefs about the world and how we must/should act or be treated, e.g. 'She must be on time', 'I should always be able to cope', 'People ought to drive at 30 mph'.	Setting rigidly high standards usually means we fail, or we are let down by others. We put ourselves and others under extreme pressure to perform, which leads to frustration, stress and anger.
EXAGGERATING	Describing a situation or a person in an over-the-top way, e.g. 'You've completely undermined my authority', 'I've ruined the weekend.'	Exaggerating (usually in a negative way) distorts the situation and causes us to feel more strongly than we need to. If I really think my authority has been swept away, my levels of upset and anger will be high.
GENERALISING	When we make sweeping statements, e.g. 'Everyone is laughing at me' or 'You are always late.'	When we generalise we ignore instances when the outcome is more positive. It also sets up a pattern where we expect the worst.
I-CAN'T-STAND-IT-ITIS	Saying or thinking that we can't bear certain things, e.g. 'I can't stand it when he raises his voice' or 'I can't bear it when people dawdle.'	Telling ourselves this reduces our ability to cope with frustrating or difficult situations. It ratchets up the stress and anger unnecessarily.

Fig. 5.2 Table of the common thinking errors

Particular thinking errors lead to particular problems. If you notice that you catastrophise a lot, your anger may be stress-related. If you personalise, your anger may be related to low self-esteem. If you suffer from I-can't-stand-it-itis, your issue is 'low frustration tolerance'. These aspects of anger will be touched on in more detail in the following chapters.

To begin with, it may seem that you don't think at all – you go straight into the feelings. That's because often the thoughts are automatic: you create them by habit and incredibly quickly. But it doesn't take a lot of practice before you can notice and adjust these automatic thoughts.

You may think that there are no thoughts involved at all. But remember that a trigger situation cannot in itself cause a feeling. That's going from A straight to C. There will always be a thinking process, even if it happens incredibly quickly.

Begin by noticing your thoughts *after* the event. Ask yourself, 'Why did I get angry?', i.e. 'What went through my head just then, before I got really angry/felt really frustrated etc?' A written record helps this process. Soon you will be noticing your thoughts as they actually happen. Then you will be able to challenge and change them.

DO IT!

Draw up an anger log for one week, preferably two. Each time you feel angry, or have an angry outburst, record the following information as soon as possible after the event:
- the trigger
- your thoughts leading up to your feeling
- your feeling(s), with a rating out of 10.

It may look like this:

A TRIGGER	B THOUGHTS	C FEELINGS / 10
Waiting at cashpoint	Why does she have to keep punching in her number? This is always happening to me!	Frustrated 7/10 Stressed 5/10
Sue asking if I'm alright	You know I'm bloody well not alright She's had enough of me complaining about work	Anger 7/10 Anxious 7/10

Note: Unless you find it really easy to identify and remember exactly what you are thinking (rare in my experience!), recording your thoughts is essential. It is only a short-term measure, until you get into the habit of noticing. You can record in a notebook, spreadsheet or on a dictaphone/MP3 player.
It's important to record your thought as precisely as possible. If you are thinking, 'She's a lazy f***' then write that down. Don't just write 'She's lazy.'

We call these thoughts in the B column 'NATs' – Negative Automatic Thoughts. They are usually unhelpful, unrealistic or illogical – or a combination of all these things. They raise the levels of your anger, stress, resentment or frustration.

NATs are unwelcome intruders in your mental airspace. They need to be picked up on the radar, challenged and turned away.

CHALLENGE YOUR NATS

Now that you have the data, use it! Identify the key NATs – the ones that are causing you most anger and frustration – and interrogate them. Ask yourself how realistic and helpful they are.

Look at how the man waiting at the cashpoint went on to challenge his NATs (Fig. 5.3). He notices the NAT (on the left) and that allows him to challenge it (on the right).

Fig. 5.3 Challenging negative automatic thoughts (NATs)

Notice how the challenge in each case turned the heat down on his anger. Notice also how the man is developing an 'internal dialogue'. Instead of just listening and acting on his automatic, exaggerated thoughts, he is bringing in the voice of calm and reason. This voice is a natural part of him (and all of us); it just needs exercising a bit more often.

By developing this internal dialogue you are creating important new habits of thinking. Eventually these habits will become as automatic as the old, unhelpful ones. You will find that you will gradually stop creating the NATs, and automatically create balanced and realistic thinking instead.

Challenging your own NATs can be difficult at first, because you assume that your thoughts are 'true'. Remember, though, that thoughts are not facts. They are mental events that *you cause*, which are your *interpretation* of events. It therefore makes sense to think things that (a) are realistic (i.e. fit the facts), and (b) are helpful (i.e. turn the heat down on your anger).

To help you, the table in Fig. 5.4 includes some useful ways in which you can challenge the common thinking errors that we identified earlier.

NAME	DESCRIPTION	CHALLENGE IT!
BLACK AND WHITE THINKING	'All or nothing' thinking, without the shades of grey	Ask yourself if the language you use really reflects reality. Imagine a spectrum rather than two poles. Think 'What's between the two extremes?'
CATASTROPHISING	Predicting the future, and expecting that to be the worst case scenario.	What is the evidence that the worst will happen? Has it always happened in the past? Think 'What's likely to happen?' 'If the worst happens, how will I deal with it?'
PERSONALISING	Taking things personally	Think of other reasons why people may be saying or doing things. Think, 'It doesn't have to be about me. S/he may be...'
BLAMING	Accusing other people, organisations or even 'life' as responsible for our problems.	Think about the part that you may have to play. Start to take a bit of responsibility – you will feel more in control and less of a victim. Think 'Is it all their fault? How am I contributing to the situation?'
MIND READING	Imagining that we know what people are thinking about us.	Why jump to conclusions without any real evidence? The thing we often imagine is what we fear, rather than what is actually happening. Think 'I'm not a mind-reader' and 'Even if they really think that, so what?'
LABELLING	Putting a (negative) global label on people.	Rate specific skills rather than the whole person. Think 'S/he's bad at ...' not 'S/he's an idiot.'
MUST-ITIS	Holding rigid beliefs about the world and how you should act or be treated.	Watch out for the 'must's, 'should's, 'ought's and 'got to's in our thoughts. Replace them with less critical and less demanding language. Think 'I would like them to...', 'It would be nice if ...'
EXAGGERATING	Describing a situation or person in an over-the-top way.	Watch your language! Is it really as bad as all that? Think 'annoying', 'damaged' – not 'dreadful', 'utterly ruined' etc.
GENERALISING	Making sweeping statements.	What about all the instances when this isn't the case? Think 'often', 'sometimes', 'some people' – not 'never', 'always' and 'everyone'.
I-CAN'T-STAND-IT-ITIS	Saying or thinking that we can't bear certain things.	Usually we can stand it. Focusing on what we can do to make it more bearable is a much more helpful thinking skill. Think 'This is difficult' not 'This is unbearable'.

Fig. 5.4 Table of challenges to the common thinking errors

DO IT!

1) Go back to the anger log that you drew up (pages 64-65). Think hard about how you could challenge your anger-creating NATs. Write down the challenges in a new column next to each one.

2) Practise identifying and challenging your NATs when you feel angry. For the next 1-2 weeks record your thoughts – and your challenges – as soon as you can after the event.

3) By the end of this period the aim is to identify and challenge your NATs as they happen, rather than after the event. Notice how this reduces your anger/ frustration level. Keep recording what you have done (after the event), and indicate the new anger level in the final column.

Note: Recording your thoughts and challenges in the short term is essential (see Note, page 65 above). If you cannot reach for your notebook/voice recorder/spreadsheet immediately then make a clear mental note at the time and record it properly later.

Draw up your anger log so that it looks like this:

A TRIGGER	B THOUGHTS (NATS)	C FEELING (ANGER)/10	D MORE HELPFUL, REALISTIC THOUGHTS	E NEW FEELING (ANGER)/10

You may find it hard to be objective about your NATs. If so, imagine that your best friend was creating these thoughts – how could you challenge him (or her)?

By challenging your NATs you are developing an internal dialogue. You are reasoning with yourself. You are navigating your ship through stormy waters to the calm of a harbour. The way in which you intervene in your habitual thought process is described in Fig. 5.5.

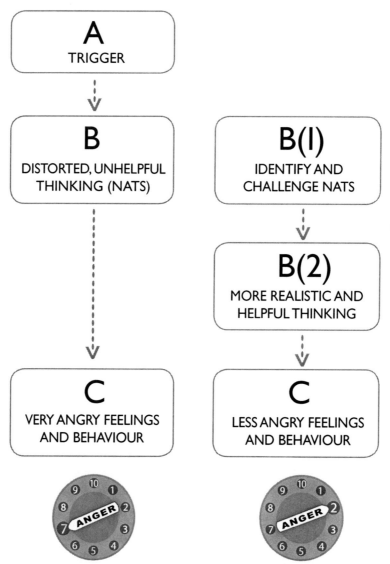

Fig. 5.5 Intervening in your thought process

By creating an internal dialogue in this way you will gradually replace old habits of thinking with new, more helpful ones. The old NATs will be less frequent and less strong. You will find that in many cases you will go straight from the trigger (A) to the more realistic and helpful beliefs (B2).

Appendix 4 gives you a checklist of questions to ask yourself when you catch yourself creating any NAT.

copymaster 36

> ## CASE STUDY
>
> Gary's anger log showed him that a lot of his angry outbursts at home were triggered by his teenage son being untidy, clumsy or careless. By noticing and recording his thoughts just before these outbursts he identified several thinking errors. He challenged and adjusted these NATs. For example he challenged 'He's a complete waste of space' with 'That's labelling – what he's done is annoying, but mostly he's OK'. He challenged 'I shouldn't have to clear up after him' with 'That's must-itis – I don't have to clear up, I am choosing to, and then getting resentful. I need to talk to him about what effect his mess has on me.'
>
> Gary managed to turn the heat of his anger down a huge amount simply by thinking in a more realistic and helpful way. Talking with his son also helped him feel he was taking control rather than acting the victim.

Sometimes it may be difficult to challenge your thoughts because on the surface they don't seem to be remarkable in any way. For example, Nick got very angry when his son questioned his request to go to bed. The surface thought may have been, 'Why is he questioning me?' However, this thought in itself is not enough to cause high levels of anger, is it? You have to dig down a bit. Actually what Nick is thinking is, 'He should not be questioning me.'

A good way of 'digging down' is the 'downward arrow' technique, when you ask what each thought actually means, or what is so bad about it. Nick above used this technique to trace his thought process to its core:

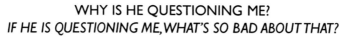

WHY IS HE QUESTIONING ME?
IF HE IS QUESTIONING ME, WHAT'S SO BAD ABOUT THAT?

IT'S BAD BECAUSE HE SHOULDN'T BE QUESTIONING ME.
SO IF HE'S BREAKING THIS RULE, WHAT'S SO BAD ABOUT THAT?

IT MEANS I DON'T HAVE ANY CONTROL OR AUTHORITY.
IF I DON'T HAVE ANY CONTROL, WHAT DOES THAT MEAN?

IT MEANS I'M WEAK.

If your thoughts are questions, reframe them as statements. If the statements don't seem to be enough to cause that level of anger, then ask yourself what is so bad about them. This will lead you more accurately to the NAT causing the anger.

By using the downward arrow technique, Nick was able to see why he got so angry. He challenged the key NAT which linked his son's questioning with his own 'weakness' by reminding himself that he wasn't weak, and that his son's questioning didn't 'make' him weak.

CHALLENGE YOUR UNWRITTEN RULES

Sometimes our thinking is based on a deeper level of thought which we may not always be aware of. These are what we could call 'assumptions'. They are unwritten rules of behaviour that we follow, often without really questioning them.

If our assumptions are unrealistic and unhelpful, then our thinking that stems from them in the actual moment will also be unrealistic and unhelpful. So we need to be aware of our assumptions, our unwritten rules, and challenge these as well.

Here are some of the common unwritten rules that angry men have:

1. I have to be tough.
2. I must always win.
3. I have to be in control at all times.
4. I must not be angry.

Notice first of all that these are all rigid rules – as such they are examples of the thinking error 'must-itis'. Rules like this can get us into terrible trouble. The example in Fig. 5.6 describes the thinking process of a man who is concerned about being late for a social event.

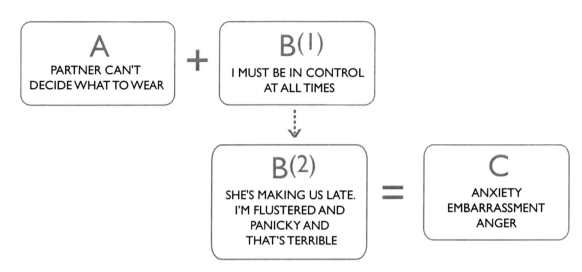

A
PARTNER CAN'T
DECIDE WHAT TO WEAR

+

B(1)
I MUST BE IN CONTROL
AT ALL TIMES

B(2)
SHE'S MAKING US LATE.
I'M FLUSTERED AND
PANICKY AND
THAT'S TERRIBLE

=

C
ANXIETY
EMBARRASSMENT
ANGER

Fig. 5.6 Example of following an
unhelpful, unwritten rule or assumption

Here the thought 'I'm flustered and panicky and that's terrible' (2) is based on the unwritten rule (1) 'I must be in control at all times'. In his mind, his partner's behaviour is causing his golden rule to be broken, and the anxiety and shame of that are enough to set off an angry reaction. (For more explanation of how anger is a reaction to loss of face, see chapter 7.)

Let's challenge some of the common unwritten rules, one by one.

1 *I have to be tough.* Macho culture has a lot to answer for. If you assume that you have to be tough, then you will err on the side of doling out criticisms when others make mistakes, unbalanced by praise for their achievements. You will resort to aggressive language and behaviour instead of assertiveness. You will be looking for a fight, and often that means getting what you look for.

Consider instead how your tough man image gets you into trouble, raises the stakes, raises the emotional temperature. Being fair-minded, complimentary, kind, flexible – these may be 'softer' virtues, but they are marks of an emotionally intelligent man, not a softie.

Try out this new rule: *'I like to be tough when it's helpful and right to be tough, but I don't have to be tough all the time.'*

2 *I must always win.* Living in a world of winners and losers, of goodies and baddies, also raises the emotional temperature. You will adopt a combative approach to any difference of opinion, instead of trying to appreciate what both sides bring to the issue.

This assumption also raises the stakes, because if you lose … what then? A huge loss of face. And that can make men very angry indeed.

Try out this new rule: *'I don't always have to win. Sometimes it is stronger and more helpful to be flexible or conciliatory.'*

3 *I have to be in control at all times.* Some men have very high standards of behaviour. Ironically this can get them into difficulties, which includes being angry. The anger is a cover for a more difficult feeling, which is not being on top of a situation. The full reasoning is, I have to be in control at all times or I am weak (remember Nick and his son?).

As men we need to accept that we cannot control everything. That things won't always work out our way. And that this doesn't reflect badly on us as human beings. When we are not in control, we are being human, not weak. We need to give ourselves a break.

Try out this new rule: *'I don't always have to be in control. Sometimes it is reasonable to be confused/unsure/vulnerable, however unpleasant this may sometimes feel.'*

4 *I must not be angry.* No, this isn't a joke. I see lots of men whose anger is provoked by a deep belief such as this. Maybe they have been brought up to believe that anger is wrong. Maybe they have been angry in the past, with disastrous results. The consequence of their belief is that they sit on their anger, feeling guilty and resentful in equal measure, until they explode with the frustration of it all.

It is a false belief. As we saw in chapter 3, anger is a natural emotion, and often it is healthy to express it. It's the way we express it that needs care and attention.

Try out this new rule: *'It's OK to feel angry. I need to express this anger in a healthy way, before it gets out of hand.'*

Identify any unwritten rules or assumptions that you hold which contribute to you being angry. Devote a page in your notebook to each one, and write about it in this way:

My old rule is:
I know this rule is in operation because:
However, the rule is unreasonable because:
The advantages of obeying this rule are:
But the disadvantages are:
A more realistic and helpful rule to follow would be:
I commit to following this new rule because:

Hussein came to realise that one of his unwritten rules was 'I have got to be tough at all times'. That's how he was brought up by his father. It meant that he could look after himself on the streets as a boy, but it got him into trouble when he began to manage a group of men at work. The only tools he used to get things done were to threaten and bully. When he met opposition, he lashed out verbally. Hussein tried out a new rule – 'I can be easy-going at times'. He found he got less angry – and got more work out of his men.

IMAGINE YOURSELF CALM

Imagery, or visualisation, can be a fantastically powerful tool in our attempts to change patterns of thought and behaviour. It involves creating a particular mental image of the situation. If the brain repeats a helpful image, where the person is represented as thinking, feeling and acting in a certain way, then it effectively primes or programmes the person to think, feel and act precisely in that way.

We can use all the learning and tools in this chapter by incorporating them into a simple visualisation technique, which can be tailor-made to your individual circumstance. It is particularly useful for preparing yourself for a situation that normally would provoke you to anger. This could be a repeated situation, such as a meeting with your boss, or it could be a one-off that you are getting worked up about.

Follow the steps in the flowchart (Fig. 5.7).

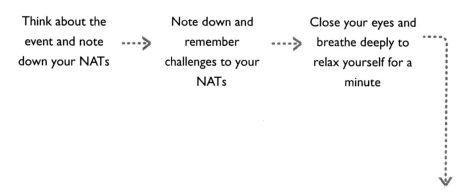

Think about the event and note down your NATs ····> Note down and remember challenges to your NATs ····> Close your eyes and breathe deeply to relax yourself for a minute

Repeat the exercise regularly in advance of the situation <···· End the visualisation on a positive note – picturing yourself coming out of the situation with much reduced levels of anger <···· Still relaxed and with eyes closed, picture the event happening. Picture yourself creating the NATs, but then responding in a balanced, helpful way – i.e. engaging in your 'internal dialogue'

Fig. 5.7 Anger-reducing imagery technique

TOOLKIT

- Learn to think in a more realistic and helpful way, as this always leads to more positive feelings and outcomes.
- It helps to identify any thinking errors that you are in the habit of making.
- Challenging your NATs (Negative Automatic Thoughts), and adjusting them so that they are more helpful and realistic, will turn the heat down on your anger.
- Challenge any assumptions or unwritten rules that you follow that make you more angry than you need to be.
- You may have to use the downward arrow technique to find what is so bad about a particular thought.
- Use imagery to prepare yourself for a situation where you would normally get angry.

learning log

WHAT I HAVE LEARNT	WHAT I CAN DO

6 | DEAL WITH IRRITATION & FRUSTRATION

AIMS
- To describe 'low frustration tolerance', or LFT, and how it causes anger
- To identify and challenge the thinking errors and NATs that lie behind LFT
- To show how problem-solving is more effective than being a victim
- To describe the links between anger and depression
- To explore how to deal with angry feelings left over from the past

In chapter 3 the two main triggers of anger were identified as irritants and loss. This chapter looks in more detail at the first of these triggers - irritants.

LFT – LOW FRUSTRATION TOLERANCE

One of the most widespread sources of anger is so common that it has its own abbreviation – LFT. Low frustration tolerance describes a state of mind where the tolerance level is very low. Our tolerance of what? Well, almost anything that could get in the way of ('frustrate') us achieving what we want, when we want.

Typical LFT triggers are:

- Waiting in queues, in shops or in traffic jams
- Being affected by your own or other people's mistakes, e.g. losing your car keys, a service engineer not turning up, braking to avoid being hit by a car
- Being affected by unforeseen circumstances, e.g. a late train, a downpour
- Being on the raw end of a malfunctioning object, such as a computer.

When our tolerance level is low, our frustration level is higher. Heightened frustration causes anger. The full cycle is described in Fig. 6.1.

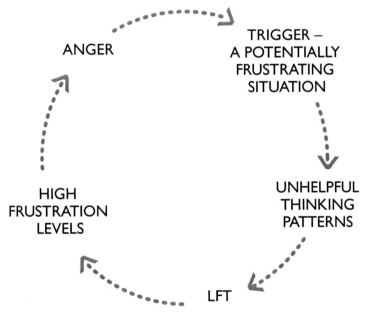

Fig. 6.1 The LFT
(low frustration tolerance) cycle

The LFT cycle is a vicious cycle because when we are angry we will respond to situations in a less tolerant way. That is, we will be even more irritated by things. Some men are in a continuous state of frustration because of LFT. Their anger is kept at simmering point, which means they are more likely to react emotionally and feel high levels of frustration.

Increased levels of anger in certain situations make us more likely to react in a similar way in other similar situations. A habit is formed – and this is the other reason why LFT is a vicious cycle. Each time we repeat the habit our brain notices the pattern and logs it. In similar situations the brain 'pattern matches', which makes it more likely that we will repeat the same behaviour. And so on.

CASE STUDY

Chris finds waiting in queues almost intolerable. He is a highly efficient and active person himself, but being the 'victim' of slow shop assistants, or of members of the public who fail to fill in their forms or find their change quickly enough, drives him to distraction. He stands in line and fumes. When he comes to be served he struggles to be civil, and carries his bad mood with him for the rest of the day. Often he abandons his wait altogether, even if that means leaving a trolley full of food. One day the till roll ran out just as he reached the counter, and he swore at the assistant. He realised then that he needed to address his anger problem.

CHALLENGING YOUR NATS

In chapter 5 we saw how the key source of your feelings is your thoughts or beliefs. We can get into the habit of generating unrealistic or unhelpful thoughts in certain trigger situations. Identifying and challenging these negative automatic thoughts (NATs) is the main way in which we can turn the temperature dial down on our anger.

So let's apply the same approach to LFT. Common NATs that we generate in frustrating situations are the following:

- I can't stand …
- People shouldn't …
- It's terrible …
- It's typical …

Let's explore these NATs one by one.

I can't stand … When we say 'I can't stand' something or 'I can't bear' someone, we immediately raise the emotional temperature and lower our frustration tolerance. Think about it: if something is unbearable then how *can* you bear it? Logically you will have to act and feel as if you can't bear it, which means you will be pretty distressed.

Actually there is very little that *we can't* stand or bear. Standing in a queue is living proof that you *can* stand it! It is more helpful to use words like 'annoying' and 'difficult' and focus on how you *can* bear it than to say 'I can't stand it…' which is clearly false.

Look at how Chris decided to challenge his 'I can't stand it' NAT while waiting in the supermarket queue (Fig. 6.2).

> I can't bear waiting in queues!

> Chris, this is 'I-can't-stand-it-itis'. Waiting here is a bit annoying, not unbearable, especially if you stop fuming. Why not check your phone while you're waiting?

Fig. 6.2 Challenging the 'I can't stand it' NAT

People shouldn't ... Men love rules. Rules give us standards to live by, and guidelines for behaviour. They make us feel safe. Unfortunately, too much of a good thing can backfire. Many of the men I see have rigid rules for their own behaviour and expect everyone else to follow those rules as well. That's asking for trouble, because rigid rules will inevitably be broken. And what then? We get angry.

We need to look closely at our rules and check out how reasonable they are, both for ourselves and for others. Replace 'people *must*' and 'they *should*' with more pragmatic language like 'I'd prefer it if...'. It's a shame that the world isn't perfect, but it helps to acknowledge that fact and put up with it just as it is.

Look at how Chris decided to challenge his 'people shouldn't' NAT while waiting in the supermarket queue (Fig. 6.3).

Cashiers shouldn't chat with customers after they've finished serving them. That means yet more delay before I'm served!

Chris, this is 'must-itis'. I may not want to chat, but for some people it's important to be sociable. And it's only a few seconds' delay. Chill out!

Fig. 6.3 Challenging the 'People shouldn't' NAT

It's terrible ... When we judge that situations are 'terrible', 'awful', 'dreadful' etc we raise the emotional temperature and reduce our ability to deal with the situation as it actually is. The thinking error here is exaggeration (see page 63).

Using exaggerated, emotive words is not only unhelpful; usually it is unreasonable as well. If you describe waiting for a minute in a queue as 'appalling', what adjective would you use to describe a real human tragedy? Get a sense of proportion!

Look at how Chris decided to challenge his 'it's terrible' NAT while waiting in the supermarket queue (Fig. 6.4).

I've got to wait while this woman fumbles for her change. This is dreadful!

Chris, you are exaggerating. Waiting a few extra seconds is a bit annoying but hardly 'dreadful'. Watch your language!

Fig. 6.4 Challenging the 'It's terrible' NAT

It's typical ... Men with LFT often expect the worst. If they notice that they get frustrated in queues, then they will be looking out for the slightest thing that may frustrate them every time they are in a queue. Thinking 'It's typical...' or 'Here we go again' or 'For ****'s sake' is our way of acknowledging that, yes, it's happened again.

But this is a self-fulfilling prophecy. The more we look for the feared thing, the more we will find it. Telling ourselves 'it's typical' only reinforces this vicious cycle. Trying instead to notice the times when it doesn't happen would help us far more.

Pick one of the situations that triggers your own LFT. Write down what it is that you expect to happen in these situations. For one week, log what actually happens. Be as objective as you can while compiling this log. Are you looking out for problems, and filtering out instances when it doesn't happen? Structure your log like this:

Situation: .... Prediction: ....

DATE	WHAT ACTUALLY HAPPENED

Look at how Chris decided to challenge his 'it's typical' NAT while waiting in the supermarket queue (Fig. 6.5).

For ****'s sake, here we go again – another person who has to pay for her shopping in loose change.

Chris, you are generalising. How often does that actually happen? You are ignoring all the times when it doesn't! And another 10 seconds isn't going to make any difference.

Fig. 6.5 Challenging the 'It's typical' NAT

DO IT!

Practise identifying and challenging your NATs in frustrating situations. For two weeks, record your thoughts – and your challenges – as soon as you can after the event. By the end of this period the aim is to identify and challenge your NATs as they happen, rather than after the event. Notice how this reduces your frustration levels, and indicate the new level in the final column.

TRIGGER	THOUGHTS (NATS)	FRUSTRATION LEVEL /10	MORE HELPFUL, REALISTIC THOUGHTS	FRUSTRATION LEVEL /10

PROBLEM-SOLVING

We can raise our frustration level even higher if we tell ourselves that we are completely powerless to do anything about the situation. Because if we tell ourselves we are powerless, then we will feel powerless. And there's nothing more frustrating than that. Especially for men, who often like to be active and 'in control'.

So watch out for NATs like 'I can't do anything about it' or 'I'm completely trapped' or 'I'll never be able to …'. Instead of fuming, do some effective problem-solving.

Problem-solving should come naturally to many men, who pride themselves on their ability to work things out. But this faculty seems to go out of the window when the emotional level is high. We need to remind ourselves of the basics of problem-solving (see Fig. 6.6).

EXPRESS THE PROBLEM IN TERMS OF A QUESTION
THAT NEEDS ANSWERING.

⋮
↓

BRAINSTORM THE POSSIBLE SOLUTIONS.

⋮
↓

EVALUATE THE SOLUTIONS BY LISTING THE
PROS AND CONS OF EACH ONE.

⋮
↓

CHOOSE THE BEST SOLUTION.

⋮
↓

IMPLEMENT IT.

Fig. 6.6 How to
problem-solve

copymaster 47

CASE STUDY

John was getting increasingly frustrated by his partner Sam's tiredness in the evenings. John came home from work energised and wanting to go out with her, but she usually just wanted to slump in front of the TV. He felt trapped. When he stayed in with her, he was resentful and bored. When he went out on his own, he felt guilty. Each time he came home, he dreaded having to make one or other of these decisions.

While brainstorming solutions, John realised that there was another option – talk to Sam about the issue. This seemed to be the best solution, though it meant being brave enough to share the problem with her. She was able to reassure him that she didn't mind him going out without her, and that her tiredness was only temporary while she was completing a difficult project at work.

DO IT!

Look back at your records and identify just one frustrating situation that you frequently encounter. Instead of dreading it in advance, suffering it while you are in it, and mulling over it ineffectually afterwards, adopt a problem-solving approach. Follow the steps in the flowchart. Be as creative as you can in your initial brainstorm – don't veto or judge any potential solution at this stage. When you come to make a choice, remember that the best solution is often the 'least worst'. But even the least worst is almost certainly better than the 'action' you are taking at the moment.

Another form of problem-solving is to make your life easier by avoiding triggers that could set off your LFT. If you don't like queuing, shop at less busy times. If you hate being caught in traffic, leave earlier so that delays do not make you late. If you 'can't stand it' when your children wake you up by coming home late, get some earplugs.

You can choose to remain a victim and complain about the consequences, but where does it get you to continue being wound up by the same old things? When you catch yourself saying or thinking, 'I have to ...', ask yourself, 'Do I have to?' Often you have a choice, because you can choose to do things differently.

copymaster 48

Replacing 'I have to…' with 'I choose to …' puts the responsibility firmly with you to take action and stop being such a victim.

FRUSTRATION AND DEPRESSION

Many of the angry men that I see are depressed. They may not look that way on the surface, but underneath they are wretched and miserable. They have lost their energy for work, or play, or sex, or even for life. They are preoccupied with thoughts about how useless they are, or how awful or pointless the world is. Everything is hard, or flat, or grey.

Just as being too angry can make you depressed, so can depression increase your anger. It can do this in two ways:

- By turning anger inwards, on yourself
- By reducing your capacity to tolerate things (LFT).

Let's look at how these two cycles work.

When you are in a low mood, you tend to create more negative and depressive thoughts. If you do this for too long, you also stop doing the things that give you pleasure or fulfilment (because, 'What's the point?'). This lowers your mood still further. You can feel both guilty and angry about this trap that you are in. The anger is turned inwards – you don't have the energy to turn it outwards, and you feel like punishing yourself for your situation. But in punishing yourself you lower your mood still further. And so it goes on (see Fig. 6.7).

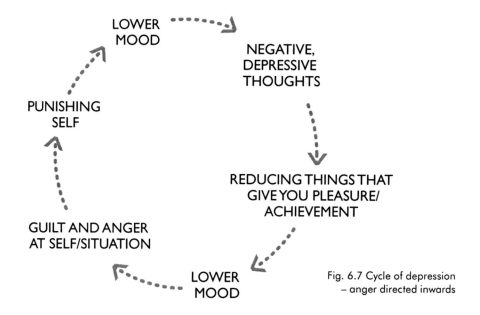

Fig. 6.7 Cycle of depression
– anger directed inwards

The second cycle is very similar. Being low and miserable lowers your tolerance to frustration. It means things you used to take in your stride become big problems or major irritants. Your lower tolerance to frustration (LFT) results in more angry outbursts. This in turn makes you more miserable because you judge yourself for being so grumpy and irritable (see Fig. 6.8).

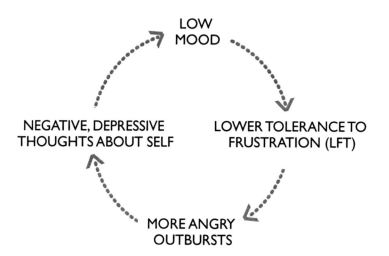

Fig. 6.8 Cycle of depression – LFT

Ian felt trapped in his work and in his personal life. His wife had left him, and was making access to his children difficult. He was under pressure to deliver more at work, but the worry and upset in his home life was preventing him from doing that. The downward spiral of his thoughts and moods led him to act in ways he had never done before, such as driving recklessly, drinking too much and, once, wrecking his kitchen.

One thing Ian's story highlights is how acts of aggressive and self-destructive behaviour are often uncharacteristic – it's his depression and desperation that drives him to express himself in this way.

If you are angry because you are depressed, then it's important to address the anger at its source. Take your depression seriously. Acknowledge it, share it with someone you trust. Read how you can help yourself. Or get professional help by seeing a therapist or visiting your doctor or health centre.

Read the checklist of common symptoms of depression below. You do not have to show all of these symptoms to be depressed. Nor do you have to show them all the time. It is more common to have bouts of depression lasting days, weeks or even months, then reverting to normal, before relapsing.

Here is a checklist of common symptoms of depression:

- Feeling low
- Loss of interest, pleasure, motivation
- Increased irritability
- Self-criticism and guilt
- Anxiety
- Pessimism
- Hopelessness
- Lack of energy
- Drastic reduction in activity, including being with people
- Changes in sleep patterns
- Loss of interest in sex
- Changes in appetite
- Difficulty in concentrating and poor memory
- Very restless or slowing right down.

GET UNSTUCK

A particular kind of frustration can result from feelings left over from the past. You may be all too aware that you are stuck with an issue, though sometimes it is difficult to work out precisely where you are stuck. Both situations lead to frustration, and often anger, because they seem to tie you down and block you from moving on as you want. Let's look at each situation in turn.

In the first kind of situation, you are stuck in the past. You may be dwelling on your relationship break-up, an unfair dismissal, a wounding attack. Whatever it is, you can't let it go. Your thoughts are dominated by 'What if...', 'If only ...',

'I should have …' and other NATs. You brood and mull, and generally work yourself up into a saucepan of simmering resentment.

If you can do something effective about the situation, then do it (see 'problem-solving' above). Often you can't, because it is ancient history. You cannot turn back the clock. All you can do is brood about it or let it go.

Which is more beneficial for you – to brood about it or let it go? It's a no-brainer.

When you catch yourself creating your stuck-in-the-past NATs, consciously challenge them: 'It's not helpful thinking like this. Let it go …'

Make a commitment to let things go that you can no longer change. To help you do this, you could visualise putting the issue in a box and storing it in your attic, out of sight. Or imagine that you are putting it in a folder, then file it away in a drawer marked 'Finished business'. A symbolic action can help this process, such as writing the issue on a piece of paper, then burning it.

In some situations it isn't immediately clear that the past is a key player in your anger. One clue is when you find yourself reacting in an over-the-top way to a person or in a particular situation. Ask yourself, 'Is this anger really about this person, or this situation?' If the answer seems to be 'No', it may be about a similar person or situation in the past. There may be some unfinished business that you need to resolve.

Tom had a new manager but found himself seething with resentment whenever she asked him to do something. He would mutter and obstruct and take his bad feelings home with him. It stopped him moving on at work, and dragged him down emotionally. In an appraisal, his manager pointed out his behaviour, and commented that his reaction to her seemed a bit childish. In a flash, Tom realised that she reminded him of his mother, who had bossed and controlled him as a child. She had since died, but making that link allowed Tom to attach his feelings to the appropriate person, and react in a less angry way to his boss.

TOOLKIT

- Challenge your LFT-creating NATs, especially those caused by the following thinking errors: I can't stand-it-itis, must-itis, exaggerating and generalising.
- Instead of feeling powerless – problem-solve.
- Consider removing or adapting the source of your frustration.
- If relevant, acknowledge that you are depressed, and do something positive about this.
- If your anger comes out of being stuck on an issue, either do something about the issue or, if that is not possible, consciously let the issue go and move on yourself.

learning log

WHAT I HAVE LEARNT	WHAT I CAN DO

copymaster 50

7 | STOP TAKING THINGS PERSONALLY

AIMS

- To explain how taking things personally and 'loss of face' lie behind a lot of men's anger
- To identify and challenge the thinking errors and NATs that contribute to this
- To describe the links between anger and low self-esteem
- To explain how perfectionism contributes to this problem.

In chapter 3 the two main triggers of anger were listed as irritants and loss. This chapter looks at the second of these triggers.

PERSONALISING

It may not seem obvious how criticism relates to *loss*. We tend to think of loss in material terms – loss of money, loss of a jacket. But for men the loss that's far and away the biggest trigger for anger is loss of face.

Loss of face can come in a variety of forms. Loss of dignity, perhaps through being teased. Loss of authority, perhaps through being 'undermined' by someone expressing a different view. Loss of approval, perhaps through being 'overlooked' for a task, job or reward.

Leo is irritable at work, at home and with his friends. When his boss mentions that they need 20% more orders next month, Leo glowers, thinking, 'He's blaming me for under performance.' When his wife points out that the dishwasher hasn't been unloaded, he snaps, 'I'm always unloading the bloody machine, why get at me?' When he suggests drinking in the Red Lion for a change but his mate says the beer there is no good, Leo fumes, thinking, 'So I know nothing about beer, do I?'

Being Leo, or being a man like Leo, is tough. Living or working with men like Leo is also tough. They are always on the defensive, always looking for the remark or action that is aimed directly at them. They seem to be strong and forceful on the outside; actually their skin is wafer thin. They are sensitive to anything that could be taken as a criticism of themselves.

Note the wording above: 'anything that *could be taken* as a criticism of themselves'. Yet again the root of the anger problem is not another person's words or actions, but the way these words or actions are interpreted. Let's go back to our A B C (see Fig. 7.1).

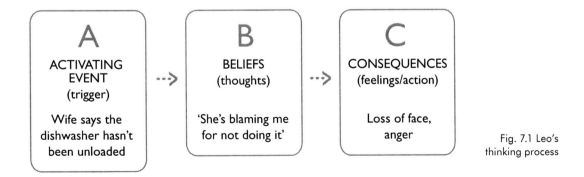

Fig. 7.1 Leo's thinking process

DO IT !

Leo responded badly to his wife, his boss and his friend. Look back at the case study and identify the precise cause of his anger in each case. Make sure you don't confuse the cause with the trigger. When you have identified the cause, think how you would advise Leo to turn the heat down on his anger.

What Leo and others like him are doing is personalising. We met this thinking error in the chart on page 63. It is one of the key causes of anger, especially among men.

Here are just some of the NATs (negative automatic thoughts) that make us personalise:

- He is blaming me for …
- He thinks I'm not working hard enough
- He is saying I've made a mistake
- She thinks I don't pull my weight
- They think I'm ignorant
- He's ignoring me
- She thinks I'm not good enough
- He thinks I can't …

The list is endless. How can you zap these NATs? Because you need to, or they will either drive you to unnecessary anger or even violence, or tip you into depression.

As always, the first step is to identify what precisely you are thinking. Then challenge it. How do you know that you are being attacked or criticised here? Aren't you in danger of that other thinking error, Mind-reading? What other views could you take about the comment or action?

Consider these possibilities:

- The person is making a descriptive or factual comment. It is a concern to them. It doesn't necessarily mean they see you as responsible for the state of affairs.

- The person is only expressing an opinion. Remember that beliefs and opinions are not facts. People are fallible; they can be wrong in their opinions. They could be under pressure, inefficient, unclear, or just had a bad day. Can you allow them to be wrong?

Fig. 7.2 describes how Leo could challenge each of the NATs that made him so angry that day.

FIX IT Toolkits for men © Kim Richardson 2010

Fig. 7.2 Leo
challenging his NATs

Taking things personally is like dropping a mallet on your toe. It hurts. It makes you sore. It makes you mad. And partly because you didn't have to do it. Imagine that your mate has passed you a mallet. What can you do?

- You can take it firmly with your right hand.
- You can take it firmly with your left hand.
- You can take it firmly with both hands.
- You can say you don't need it right now.
- You can ask him to put it down near you.
- You can take it and drop it on your toe.

There are several ways you can act. Choosing to take a comment or behaviour personally is like choosing to drop the mallet on your toe.

So when you find yourself personalising, apply the mallet test. Think, 'How else could I interpret the situation?' That way you will not drop the mallet on your toe.

For one week, be hyper-aware of how you may be taking things personally. Note down the triggers, your thoughts and your feelings in the usual way. Challenge the NATs. Make a mental note at the time, then fill the table in later. Even if you do not succeed to challenge the NATs in the moment, doing a thought record like this after the event will help you challenge personalising in the heat of the moment in future instances. Notice how often you drop that mallet on your toe, and what you can do instead.

Often when we personalise, we are taking ourselves too seriously. Did your co-worker really have you in mind when he made that comment? Are you really on top of his list of concerns? Did your friend really care so much about your opinion that they set out to rubbish it?

We are not as central in other people's lives as we think we are. We need to take our ego out of the equation. We need to relax, take a step back and view the situation a bit more dispassionately.

This also applies to responding to teasing and jokes. If these are meant as genuine attempts to be funny, then take them that way. If you expect people to have as their main aim to put you down, then you need to be responsible for the consequences, which are upset and anger on your part.

Think about how you are coming across – bad-tempered, over-sensitive, suspicious, boring. Is that how you want to be perceived? If someone responded angrily to a tease of your own, what would *you* think of *him*?

This chapter tackles perceived criticism – when we think (often wrongly) that we are being criticised. Sometimes, of course, we are on the end of actual criticism, malicious teasing, or even aggression. Responding in a non-angry way to these behaviours is covered in chapter 8 on Assertiveness.

WHEN SELF-CRITICISM MEANS LOW SELF-ESTEEM

Many of the angry men I see in my practice are angry because they have low self-esteem. They disguise this from themselves (and others) by getting explosively angry, but this only covers up a deeper hurt. They hurt because they feel bad, inadequate, not up to the job, rejected, a failure.

How does this work? Look at this example. Andy explodes with anger one day when his wife complains that the central heating still doesn't work properly and she's cold. The thought, 'She's criticising me' didn't seem to be powerful enough to explain the level of anger that followed. In cases like this we have to do a bit of detective work, digging around to find out what the actual thought is that causes the feeling (hurt and anger).

A good way of doing this is the 'downward arrow' technique, when you ask what each thought actually means, or what is so bad about it. it (see page 72 above). Andy used this technique to trace his thought process to its core (see Fig. 7.3).

SHE IS BLAMING ME FOR FIXING THE CENTRAL HEATING.
IF YOU HAVEN'T FIXED IT, WHAT'S SO BAD ABOUT THAT?

IT MEANS I HAVEN'T DONE A JOB PROPERLY.
IF YOU HAVEN'T DONE A JOB PROPERLY, WHAT DOES THAT MEAN?

IT MEANS I'M
INADEQUATE.

Fig. 7.3 The downward arrow technique – Andy

Note that Brian, in exactly the same situation, doesn't get so angry because his 'bottom line' is very different (Fig. 7.4).

SHE IS BLAMING ME FOR FIXING THE CENTRAL HEATING
IF YOU HAVEN'T FIXED IT, WHAT'S SO BAD ABOUT THAT?

IT MEANS I HAVEN'T DONE A JOB PROPERLY
IF YOU HAVEN'T DONE A JOB PROPERLY, WHAT DOES THAT MEAN?

IT MEANS I CAN'T GET EVERYTHING RIGHT.
I'M ONLY HUMAN. I'LL HAVE ANOTHER GO.

Fig. 7.4 The downward arrow technique – Brian

The downward arrow technique is very useful when you want to get to the bottom of your anger. If your conscious thought doesn't seem to justify the level of anger that you are feeling, then ask yourself, 'What does that thought mean?', 'What's so bad about that?' or 'Why does that matter?' Keep asking yourself this question until you reach a conclusion that does justify the level of anger. That is the underlying cause of your anger, and that is what needs examining and challenging.

Men who think they are inadequate often feel very hurt. And men who feel very hurt often cover that hurt by being angry. Anger both expresses the hurt and covers it up by turning the critical attention onto the other person. But that only serves to add a separate problem onto the first (see Fig. 7.5).

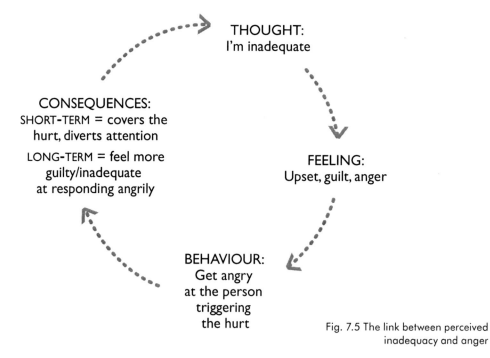

THOUGHT:
I'm inadequate

CONSEQUENCES:
SHORT-TERM = covers the
hurt, diverts attention

LONG-TERM = feel more
guilty/inadequate
at responding angrily

FEELING:
Upset, guilt, anger

BEHAVIOUR:
Get angry
at the person
triggering
the hurt

Fig. 7.5 The link between perceived
inadequacy and anger

If you are constantly running up against the thought that you are a failure or inadequate, then you need to work on your self-esteem. Instead of rubbishing yourself for not being able to do something, take the whole picture into account. Be fair to yourself. Give yourself some slack.

The men who I see in my practice often have incredibly high standards of behaviour. The problem is that they generally apply these standards to themselves rather than others. So they actually have double standards. They are biased against themselves.

That's a double whammy. On the one hand they are critical of themselves for not being Superman. On the other hand they see criticism of themselves in every casual comment or action of others. No wonder they feel beaten. No wonder they react with hurt and anger.

CASE STUDY

Darren was brought up to think that he couldn't get anything right. His father savagely criticised him for the smallest of faults, and never praised him. In his adult life Darren developed a tough man exterior, but underneath felt that everyone was out to get him. He dealt with this by fighting back – attacking as a form of defence. He lost jobs, friends, partners. He came to realise that his single biggest critic was himself, and he worked on accepting himself instead of continuing the family tradition of undermining himself. As his self-acceptance rose, his anger levels fell.

STOP BEING A PERFECTIONIST

A special form of self-criticism is perfectionism. Men who follow a rule that says, 'Everything I do has to be perfect' are often actually fearful of failure. They fear failure because in their mind that means they *are* failures. So they chase their own tails, aiming for 100% perfection. Only that way will they 'prove' to themselves that they are not really failures.

Of course, perfectionism is a savage master. It's a slave driver. By being a perfectionist you work exceptionally hard at all times to prevent the dreaded 'failure'. That can lead to stress, burn-out, frustration. You are also setting yourself up for failure, because no one can be perfect. So you cause the very thing you fear.

Pin the phrase 'FEEDBACK NOT FAILURE' on your notice board or on the fridge. When you do something wrong, see what you can learn from it. That way you will improve and move on.
Instead, if you simply call yourself a failure, you will beat yourself up, feel bad and perform worse. Which is the better response – feedback or failure?

copymaster 55

The remedy for perfectionism is self-acceptance. Note that self-acceptance is not the same thing as putting up with low standards. Men with high standards are terrified of 'losing' these standards, as if the world would come to an end if the perfectionist rule were adjusted slightly. Actually self-acceptance means accepting the fact that you are a human being, with good points, bad points and neutral points. You will keep working on your bad points. But having bad points does not make you useless or inadequate. This is to fall foul of two dangerous thinking errors - Labelling and Black and White Thinking (see page 63).

If you accept others for not being perfect, why not accept yourself?

copymaster 56

If you think you are a perfectionist, you need to challenge your beliefs.

1) Write down any specific perfectionist beliefs that you hold, e.g. 'I have to get everything right or I'll be criticised' or 'If something is worth doing, it's worth doing perfectly.'

2) Take each one in turn and write down the advantages and disadvantages of holding the belief. Think about things like fairness, the effect on how you see yourself, the effect on your energy, workload and relationships.

3) If you think that the disadvantages outweigh the advantages, try adjusting the belief so that it is more helpful and/or realistic.

4) Now apply the new belief consciously in your life.

For example, you could change a belief 'If I make a mistake, then I'm bad' into 'If I make a mistake I will try to learn from it, but it doesn't mean I'm a bad person.'

TOOLKIT

- Don't automatically take things personally by assuming you are being criticised or to blame. Personalising is a major cause of angry feelings.
- Personalising usually also involves mind-reading, another thinking error. We do not know what people are thinking, or the real motivation behind their words or actions.
- Choose to take a different perspective on the words or actions. Do not choose to drop a mallet on your toe.
- Remember that people aren't generally as concerned about you as you think. You are not that important!
- Use the 'downward arrow' technique to work out the core belief that is causing the anger.
- If your core belief is that you are inadequate or a failure, then work on accepting yourself.
- Never label yourself a failure. Instead, say 'I made a mistake'. Remember – 'Feedback not failure'.
- Apply the same standards of behaviour to yourself as you do to others.
- Challenge your perfectionist beliefs. They are not a sign that you are perfect – they mean you fear failure.

learning log

WHAT I HAVE LEARNT	WHAT I CAN DO

8 | BE ASSERTIVE

AIMS

- To explore how being passive often results in anger and aggression
- To describe assertive communication and behaviour, and distinguish it from passive and aggressive behaviour
- To explore the advantages of assertiveness over other forms of communication and behaviour
- To challenge common assumptions that lie behind not adopting assertive behaviour
- To outline the basic three-step model of assertiveness
- To explore how best to deal with criticism and conflict

HOW BEING PASSIVE RESULTS IN ANGER AND AGGRESSION

Many angry men have a problem being assertive. Indeed, it is often their non-assertiveness that results in their angry outbursts. The traditional view is that it is loud, aggressive and pushy men who have an anger problem. In my experience it is often the opposite. When men are passive and do not speak out – that's where the trouble often lies.

How does being quiet and passive result in the opposite, anger and aggression? Very easily. For several reasons, men can find it hard to ask for what they want. Men who don't express their needs deny their needs. This leads to both resentment and frustration: resentment that their needs aren't being met, and frustration with themselves.

The more these men suppress their needs, the more the resentment and frustration grow. The result is usually an explosion of anger, accompanied by aggressive language and behaviour.

And the consequence of that? Further 'evidence' that if they ask for what they want, disaster follows. It's another vicious circle:

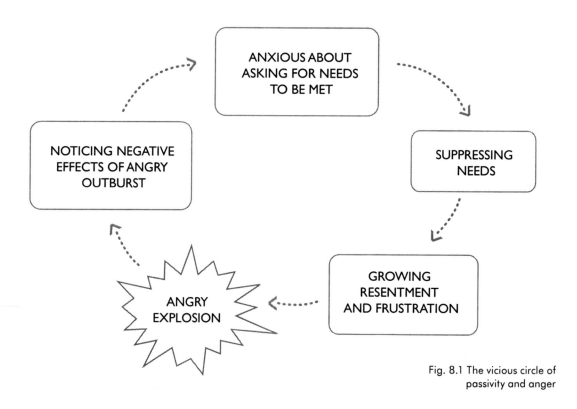

Fig. 8.1 The vicious circle of passivity and anger

Rob's school-age stepson, Charlie, has developed the habit of doing his homework in front of the television. He spreads his books over the sofa and fires questions at his mother. Rob has taken to giving up watching TV and instead retreats to his study where he works or plays computer games. But underneath he feels excluded and fed up. One day, when his favourite programme is on he can't contain himself and yells at Charlie to go to his room. The argument escalates and draws in his wife. Rob gets his seat in front of the TV but is too worked up and ashamed to enjoy the programme.

We will explore later on what stops men asking for what they want. But for the moment let us consider the main problem. There seems to be no middle ground between being passive and being aggressive. Men like Rob bounce between one and the other, getting satisfaction from neither. They alternately frustrate and intimidate their colleagues, friends and family.

However, there is something between passivity and aggression – it's called assertiveness.

WHAT IS ASSERTIVE BEHAVIOUR?

Before defining assertiveness, let's list what assertiveness looks and sounds like in practice. A useful way of doing this is to set it alongside passive and aggressive behaviour. (Note: the table below also includes passive-aggressive behaviour, which (unsurprisingly) is a mixture of the passive and aggressive behaviours.)

	COULD BE DESCRIBED AS …	NON-VERBAL SIGNALS YOU MAY GIVE	KEY WORDS AND PHRASES YOU MAY USE
AGGRESSIVE	demanding, arrogant, blaming, insulting, pushy, loud, uncompromising	shouting, raised voice, pointing, folded arms, standing over	You …, You'd better …, If you don't …, Should, Bad, insults
PASSIVE	victim, subservient, loser, avoiding, cowardly, powerless, weak, ineffective	whining or little voice, shuffling feet, downcast eyes, silence	I'm sorry, I wonder, I hope you don't mind (or silence)
PASSIVE-AGGRESSIVE	manipulative, powerless, martyr, judgemental, pressurising, emotional bribery	clenched jaw, avoiding the other, slamming doors, withdrawing, silence, sulking	muttering to yourself, sarcasm (or silence)
ASSERTIVE	direct, honest, respectful, listening, effective, empowering	calm and controlled voice, relaxed posture, direct eye contact	'I' statements, I think, I feel, I want, How can we resolve this?, What do you think?

Fig. 8.2 Comparing assertive, aggressive, passive and passive-aggressive behaviours and communication

DO IT!

Look at the table of behaviours. When you want something done, or when you want to challenge or question others, which kind of behaviour do you generally choose? Note that you may choose one kind of behaviour in one environment, e.g. at home, and another behaviour in another environment, e.g. at work.

Assertiveness describes a certain kind of behaviour. It is behaviour which helps us communicate clearly and confidently our needs, wants and feelings. It is an alternative to passive, aggressive and manipulative (passive-aggressive) behaviour.

When we are assertive, we decide what we want, decide if it is fair, ask clearly for it, and in a calm and relaxed manner. We express our feelings openly, and can give and take both compliments and criticism. Assertiveness does not mean shouting, bullying, calling people insulting names, putting people down, bottling up our feelings or beating about the bush.

In particular, do not confuse an assertive person with the stereotypical 'pushy' person. Assertiveness is about respect – respecting our own needs and respecting the other's needs to be treated properly. Being pushy is usually being aggressive, because it is pressurising.

Note that being assertive does not necessarily get you what you want. It is a way of communicating your needs openly, honestly and respectfully. Although it is often the most likely means of getting what you want, it equally often leads to compromise or negotiation rather than an outright win for one party. It is a win-win approach.

Being assertive is based on an acceptance that we have the right to assert our needs. In particular we (and all others) have these rights:

- The right to ask for what we want (realising that the other person has the right to say No)
- The right to have an opinion and feelings and to express them appropriately
- The right to make mistakes or be imperfect
- The right to change our mind

DO IT!

1) Read the assertiveness rights above. Mark the ones that you find it difficult to accept. Why do you find it/them difficult to accept?

2) What are the consequences of denying yourself these rights? For example, do they stop you getting what you want out of life?

3) Do you accept these rights for other people? If so, why not for yourself?

Be careful to distinguish between feeling confident about saying something and having the right to say it. Just because you feel anxious about the outcome of speaking up does not mean you do not have the right to speak up. But unless you believe you have the right, you will never develop the confidence to express that right in practice.

WHAT STOPS MEN ASKING FOR WHAT THEY WANT?

Many men find it hard to accept that they have the right to ask for what they want. Others accept this right, but still struggle with exercising it. This is because they make certain assumptions about assertiveness, or about their capacities. These assumptions may not be conscious thoughts, but they need challenging all the same. (For more about assumptions see page 73 above.)

Some of the key assumptions are the following:

- 'I can't be assertive – I don't have the skills.'
- 'It's wrong to ask for what you want.'
- 'Something bad will happen if I ask for what I want.'

Let's address these assumptions one by one.

1 *'I can't be assertive – I don't have the skills.'*

If you have never actually asked for what you want in a reasonable, respectful way, then you are likely to assume that you cannot do it. But there are at least two things wrong with this assumption.

One false assumption is that we have *never* been assertive. There are always cases where we have asked for what we want – we have just filtered this information out, or discounted it because it belongs to another realm of our life (e.g. we've been assertive at work, but we assume that we cannot be assertive because we can't ask for what we want at home).

Secondly, it is just plain illogical to say that because we *don't* do something therefore we *can't* do something. What would you reply to a son of yours who said, 'I can't swim'? We gain our skills and our confidence through practice. Expecting to have skills and confidence in anything before we actually do it is putting the cart before the horse.

Try out this new rule: *'I find it difficult at the moment to be assertive in this particular area but if I practise I will gain confidence.'*

2 *'It's wrong to ask for what you want.'*

Many men find the very idea of asking for something difficult. It may be that it makes them vulnerable. Or that it's selfish and demanding to ask for their needs to be met. Or they have another assumption – that they shouldn't have to ask; it should be given.

copymaster 61

copymaster 62

If you are one of these men, the precise challenge that you need to make to this assumption depends on the precise reason why you think being assertive is 'wrong'. (See the *Do it!* box below.) One way of cutting through this knotty problem is to imagine someone asking you, in a clear but respectful way, for something that they want. Would you say that they were 'wrong' to ask? (Remember that you have the right to deny their request, or negotiate – see the table of rights above.)

So, if it isn't wrong for someone else, how can it be wrong for you?

Try out this new rule: *'It may feel wrong to ask for what I want, but that doesn't make it wrong. I have the right to be assertive, just as others do.'*

If you think that asking for your needs to be met is wrong, then do this exercise.

1) Think of a time recently when you stopped yourself being assertive – when you didn't ask for what you wanted.

2) Replay the tape of the event in your mind, but this time with you actually asking for what you wanted.

3) What thought or image comes up for you? If it is simply, 'This is wrong', then ask yourself, 'What is bad about it?' You will then find the real reason. This may be a rigid 'rule' that you can then challenge. Or you may discover that you are fearful of the outcome, in which case you need to deal with the fear. (See page 119.)

Pete was getting worked up about his reception by his wife when he returned home from work each day. Instead of greeting him and chatting about the day, as they used to, she would now continue with her own activities, which often revolved around attending to the children. Pete wanted more attention, but found it impossible to ask for it – 'It's not right,' he thought. Instead of engaging with her, he withdrew in anger and frustration.

Eventually he forced himself to question this assumption. He imagined himself chatting to her, and noticed that he was almost shouting to himself, 'She should be doing this with me!' Challenging this rule was easy – Pete realised that he needed to play a part in the communication as well, and raise the issue if it was troubling him.

3 'Something bad will happen if I ask for what I want.'

This is a common fear. What if I am not liked? What if it provokes an argument or conflict? Often this fear is based on past experience – but past experience of aggression rather than assertiveness. Asking assertively means asking calmly and respectfully – is that the kind of asking that you did before? And did you remain assertive if the request was taken badly?

It is true that you cannot control other people's reactions. They may decide to respond very negatively. But (a) you may like to test this prediction out, and (b) you cannot be responsible for others' behaviour. If they choose to respond aggressively they have to take responsibility for that.

The bottom line is that almost always something 'bad' happens when you *don't* ask for what you want – the consequences are described in the vicious circle drawn at the beginning of this chapter. Being assertive, by contrast, empowers you, respects both you and others, and often actually gets you what you want into the bargain.

Try out this new rule: *'It may feel scary to ask for what I want, but it's the most likely way to get a positive result all round. I have the right to be assertive, just as others do.'*

HOW TO BE ASSERTIVE, NOT AGGRESSIVE

The basic model to follow when being assertive is very straightforward. It means taking three key steps:

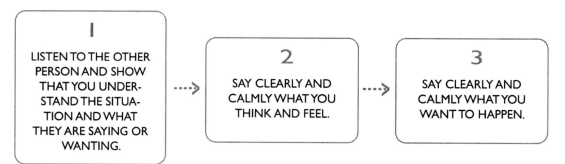

Fig. 8.3 The three-step model of assertiveness

Above all, **don't lose your temper**, because this will not result in clear communication, only escalation of any conflict. If you feel yourself losing control, take some deep breaths and count to 10 before speaking. You **cannot** be assertive if you are aggressive.

Steps one and two are crucial. Step one immediately takes the sting out of potential conflict because it develops empathy. Listen attentively and show that you have heard and understood where the other person is coming from.

Step two is communicating your message in a clear but respectful way. This often means using 'I statements' such as 'I am annoyed that you are often late' or 'I find it hard when you are late'. Using 'You statements' is often blaming, unhelpful and aggressive, e.g. 'You are always late', 'You're making me angry' etc.

Step three is often helpful because it communicates what you would like to happen, rather than simply criticising the present situation. It is constructive and provides a basis for a response, or negotiation.

CASE STUDY

The next time Rob (see page 113) wants to watch TV in peace, he sits down opposite his stepson and addresses him calmly but clearly. 'Charlie, I know you've got into the habit of doing your homework in front of the telly, but I would really like to watch my programme in peace. It's hard to do that when your books are everywhere and you're talking to your mum. Please could you tidy up here and either do your homework in your room or sit quietly over there.' Charlie gathered up his books and stomped off.

MANAGING ANGER AND IRRITATION

DO IT!

Read the case study.

1) Identify the three steps of assertiveness in Rob's request.

2) In what way was Rob (a) respecting his own needs, and (b) respecting Charlie?

3) When Charlie stomped off, who was responsible for his aggrieved feelings, Rob or Charlie? What could Rob helpfully tell himself about Charlie's reaction as he settles down to watch his programme?

copymaster 65

Remember that practice is essential. It is difficult to be confident at asking for what you want without practice. You can practice both in your head, using imagery, and in the real world.

We have already discussed the benefits and power of visualisation, or working with imagery (see pages 77-78). You can use this technique to prepare yourself for any situation that requires assertiveness. Follow the steps in the flowchart below, and repeat the exercise regularly in advance of the situation.

copymaster 66

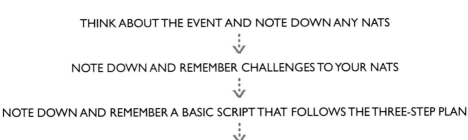

THINK ABOUT THE EVENT AND NOTE DOWN ANY NATS

NOTE DOWN AND REMEMBER CHALLENGES TO YOUR NATS

NOTE DOWN AND REMEMBER A BASIC SCRIPT THAT FOLLOWS THE THREE-STEP PLAN

CLOSE YOUR EYES AND BREATHE DEEPLY TO RELAX YOURSELF FOR A MINUTE

STILL RELAXED AND WITH EYES CLOSED, PICTURE YOURSELF IN THE SITUATION. PICTURE YOURSELF SAYING WHAT YOU WANT TO SAY, IN A CLEAR AND CALM WAY

PICTURE A NEGATIVE RESPONSE FROM THE OTHER PERSON, AND THEN YOUR OWN CLEAR AND CALM RESPONSE TO THAT, E.G. REPEATING THE MESSAGE.

END THE VISUALISATION ON A POSITIVE NOTE – PICTURING YOURSELF COMING OUT OF THE SITUATION WITH NO ANGER AND YOUR MESSAGE HAVING BEEN HEARD.

Fig. 8.4 Imagery technique to prepare for assertiveness

This imagery technique deliberately asks you to imagine 'the worst' happening, i.e. a negative response to your request. This is so that you can programme your brain to respond appropriately and effectively if that does happen. You may like to vary the possible responses in your visualisation. Each time you picture yourself responding calmly and assertively you will make it more likely to turn this into reality. However, it is important that you end the visualisation on a positive note.

It is also important to practise being assertive in the real world. But resist jumping in at the deep end and attempting to tackle those unmet needs and lingering resentments that you have been brewing over for years. Start small. Take a mouldy cabbage back to the grocer's. Ask for your coffee to be reheated. Phone your supplier and ask when they are going to pay your latest invoice.

DO IT!

Your problem being assertive may relate to particular people or situations. So begin by listing all your assertiveness problems. Be as precise as you can, e.g. 'Criticising people in authority' or 'Asking my children to help in the home'. Then rank all your assertiveness problems in order of importance or difficulty. You need to feel confident and to get the taste of success, so start at the bottom of the list and work up. Reward yourself when you manage to be assertive – let the feelings in. Learn what you could do better if things go wrong.

There are lots of individual techniques and skills that you can learn and practise to make the three-step model even more effective. Read Appendix 5, which lists ten assertiveness techniques.

DEALING WITH CRITICISM AND CONFLICT

Men are often angry and aggressive when they are on the end of criticisms or put-downs. Before we explore this area, however, we need to look briefly at the situation when they are the criticiser, as this too can lead to anger and aggression.

Some men find it hard to criticise. They may suppress the criticism, in which case the other's person behaviour or action does not change, and they themselves feel ineffective, resentful and frustrated. We have already explored some of the (false) assumptions that lie behind suppressing criticism.

Alternatively, men can link giving criticism with being angry. They get very heated, and deliver the criticism in an angry and aggressive way. They may get the other person to change their behaviour or action, but at a cost. The cost is the other person's respect and good will, as well as damage to their own sense of self, if not their health.

Remembering these key points will help you give criticism assertively rather than aggressively:

- Check out that your criticism is fair.
- Remind yourself that you have the right to ask for something, and that they have the right to say No.
- Deliver the criticism assertively, in a calm, clear way.
- Criticise the thing that they are doing, not the person. The more specific the criticism is, the less likely it is that the person will feel attacked and labelled.
- Listen to any feedback from the person criticised. Don't just dump the criticism and leave. Deal with any feedback in a clear, assertive way.

Remember that the purpose of criticism is to change someone's behaviour or action, i.e. it is **constructive**. Angrily putting someone down is **destructive**, and thus works against your goal.

Absorbing and implementing the advice in the last few paragraphs should go a long way towards helping you when you are at the other end of the stick – receiving criticism. To begin with, remind yourself that others have the right to ask for what they want – and that you have the right to say No.

You may decide the criticism is unfair. In this case, you need to disagree with the criticism assertively, which means clearly and calmly. Remember that even though

copymaster 68

copymaster 69

they may be wrong, they still have the right to make the criticism. (Everyone has the right to be wrong!) On the other hand, there is often a grain of truth in any criticism - recognising that will help you give an assertive rather than an aggressive response.

It is also important to focus on the content of the criticism, and regard it as a criticism of an action or behaviour, not of your whole person. You have a choice as to how you interpret the criticism, as you can see from Fig. 8.5. Choosing the left-hand route focuses on 'failure' and personalises the criticism. It results in higher levels of anger and frustration than choosing the right-hand route, which is balanced and constructive.

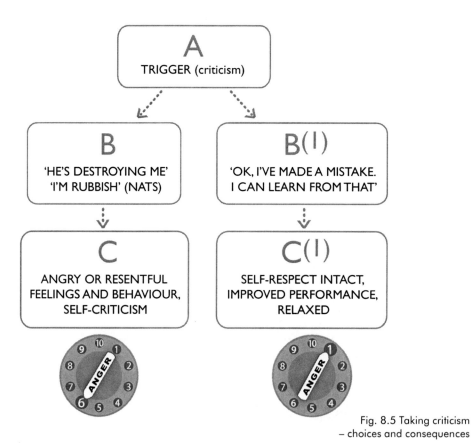

Fig. 8.5 Taking criticism
– choices and consequences

Men (and women) are more likely to respond with anger if the criticism they receive is delivered in a non-assertive way, i.e. if it is a personal attack or a put-down. But ask yourself – just because the other person is being aggressive, does that mean I have to be aggressive back?

Follow these guidelines for dealing with put-downs:

- Focus on the content of the criticism, not the emotional way it is delivered.
- Ask for more information or evidence to validate the criticism if necessary.
- State clearly that although you may agree, or at least hear, the criticism, you regard it as a put down and therefore unhelpful.
- Stick to your points assertively, in a calm, clear way.

It is very tempting to respond to an emotionally charged criticism with anger. But that is getting hooked onto the emotion, and the consequences are almost always negative. Instead of getting hooked onto the emotion, focus on the content. Your response is then more likely to be assertive rather than aggressive. Fig. 8.6 is a visual example of the choices that Graham has when he responds to an aggressive criticism of an idea he put forward at work.

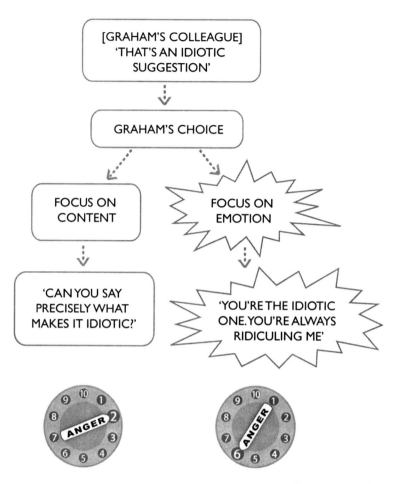

Fig. 8.6 Responding to a put-down
– choosing to focus on content or emotion

In choosing to focus on the content of the criticism Graham can remain relatively calm, and ask for clarification. He will be perceived in the meeting as the one who is mature and in control. He will also be able to assess whether his idea really is a non-starter, because he is not attaching his self-esteem to it.

If Graham chooses to get hooked onto his colleague's emotion, there is a very different outcome. He allows the criticism to relate to himself as a person, then personalises back. He has lost control, and any valid criticism of his idea goes out of the window, hidden in the smoke and fire of the developing conflict.

Look at Fig. 8.6 again. Write out the trigger (A), thoughts (B) and consequences (feelings and behaviour – C) for each of the two routes that Graham could choose.

- Identify your own predominant pattern of communication and behaviour. Make a commitment to changing your habit and becoming assertive.
- Remind yourself that you have the right to ask for your needs to be met, as long as you do this respectfully, and as long as you allow the other the right to say No.
- Identify and challenge any false and negative assumptions that you have about assertiveness.
- Follow the three-step model: 1 Listen to the other person, 2 Say clearly and calmly what you think and feel, 3 Say clearly and calmly what you want to happen.
- Practise being assertive, taking small steps first and using visualisation.
- Be calm and fair when delivering criticism – it is a constructive activity.
- When receiving criticism, separate the content from the emotion.
- When receiving a put-down, do not get hooked onto the other's emotion.

copymaster 71

learning log

WHAT I HAVE LEARNT	WHAT I CAN DO

9 | DE-STRESS YOURSELF

AIMS

- To explain the link between anger and stress
- To describe what stress is, and how our responses to it can make us more stressed
- To explore how we can change our physical responses to stress, focusing on relaxation, exercise and diet
- To explore how we can change our behavioural responses to stress, focusing on procrastination and work-life balance
- To explore how we can change our psychological responses to stress, focusing on thinking skills, assumptions and humour

ANGER AND STRESS

I see a lot of men whose anger is stress-related. When I say 'stress related' I mean that there is a connection between their anger and their stress. The connection goes both ways. People who are stressed display many and varied symptoms, but one of these is a greater tendency to anger and aggression. Likewise, when we are angry or aggressive we are more likely to raise our levels of stress – as well as raise the stress level of others around us. It is a self-fuelling cycle:

RAISED LEVEL OF STRESS   RAISED LEVEL OF ANGER

Fig. 9.1 The relationship between anger and stress

So what exactly is stress? The term is grossly overused in today's fast-moving and demanding society. Often it is used as a synonym for 'tired' or 'difficult', as in 'I've had a stressful journey' or 'Mealtimes are always stressful.'

True stress, however, is a legacy of the 'fight or flight' response – the primitive, automatic reaction that humans have to situations of severe danger. In such situations our brains and our bodies act to save us. Our heart beats faster, for example, to pump more blood to our muscles, so that we can launch ourselves into possibly life-saving action. Our adrenalin level rockets to put us on high alert. And so on.

But the 'stress response', as it is called, kicks in just as powerfully now, in 21st century Western society, as it did millennia ago when life truly was precarious. So our natural defence mechanism more often than not becomes a danger in its own right. Because the symptoms of stress are themselves severe. These symptoms can be seen in the way in which we respond physically, the way we respond in terms of our behaviour, and the way in which we think and feel (our psychological response):

Physical responses to stress.

Many of the physiological symptoms of stress are signs of the nervous system responding to what it perceives as extreme danger. Thus there is a decrease of blood flow to the digestive system (as it is less important in an emergency), and a corresponding increase of blood to the heart, leg and arm muscles. The heart pumps faster, and we sweat more. There can be a decrease in saliva, leading to dry mouth, and an increase in lung activity – quick shallow breathing rather than relaxed deep breathing. People under stress can also get indigestion, diarrhoea and tension headaches.

Behavioural responses to stress.

Some people under stress will take comfort in eating or drinking excessively. Although the former is called comfort eating, it can actually lead to discomfort as the foods are often high in fat or salt. Likewise taking to drink can also be detrimental and increase stress. Drinking coffee is another common symptom. The way we relate to others is also affected by stress: for example, people under stress may exhibit aggressive or passive aggressive behaviour. They may be irritable and moody, or develop nervous tics. Their time management may suffer, and their work performance also may be affected.

Psychological responses to stress.

When people are stressed, their perception of events is often distorted. They may dwell on negative images or pictures of situations getting out of control. They may indulge in unhelpful thinking errors such as catastrophising or must-itis. They often get depressed or feel low; sometimes they are anxious instead (or as well). Others get very angry. Sometimes these feelings of anxiety and depression can be accompanied by guilt, and often people under stress have a poor self-image. In extreme cases stress can lead to breakdown or psychosis.

List the situations, thoughts, people or events that stress you. These are the 'triggers' for your stress. In the right-hand column identify how you know they are causing you stress, ie what symptoms are you noticing? Refer back to the list of symptoms above to help you. Draw up your table like this:

STRESS TRIGGERS	STRESS SYMPTOMS
Son playing loud music	angry thoughts, pacing up and down

One striking factor in all of the above symptoms of stress is that they actually make us *more stressed*. For example, overworking in response to impossible deadlines will often lead to negative thinking and feeling and reduced sleep, pleasure and relaxation. Thus the stress cycle is itself a vicious cycle where our reactions to stress actually make our lives more stressful (see Fig. 9.2).

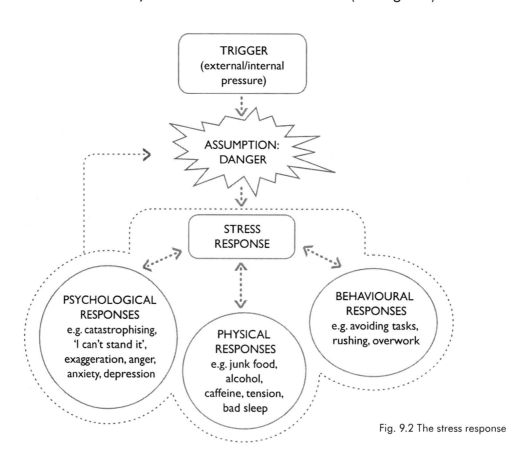

Fig. 9.2 The stress response

Keith had worked his way almost to the top of his financial services firm before he was suddenly made redundant. Even though his redundancy package was substantial and his skills and experience meant that he was likely to get a new job, Keith became obsessed with job seeking. He spent almost every moment of the day searching for jobs, applying for jobs, preparing presentations and attending interviews. Driven by the fear of 'losing everything' he let go of the few pleasurable things that he used to do, including going to the gym, and his sleep was badly affected. He was on such a short fuse that angry and irritable outbursts in the home became the norm, and made life even more intolerable both for him and his family.

Read the case study about Keith.

1) Identify (a) what triggers Keith's stress reaction, (b) what assumption he makes about the trigger, and (c) the psychological, physical and behavioural stress responses that he shows. How do his responses help or hinder his situation?

2) When his wife complains at yet another angry outburst, Keith blames his 'stress' for his anger. Is he right?

Just as men have to take responsibility for their anger, so they must also take responsibility for their stress reactions (including anger). So Keith is certainly not right to blame 'stress' for his outbursts. It is more accurate to see stress as the trigger for his anger.

135

As stress is not an external factor but a response to external factors, then the way to combat stress is to change our responses. We can do this in all of the three key areas above. So when you 'feel stressed' you don't have to just accept this as something you have no control over. Instead you can:

- Change your physical response
- Change your behaviour
- Change your thinking and feeling (psychological response).

CHANGE YOUR PHYSICAL RESPONSE

Exercise. Exercise is a fabulous stress-buster. It clears the toxic stress hormones from your bloodstream and adds pleasurable chemicals called endorphins. Regular exercise boosts your circulatory and immune systems and strengthens your body. It also aids sleep. Finally, it takes us out of ourselves and is often a sociable way of relating to friends.

When we are stressed one of the first casualties seems to be exercise. 'I haven't got time/money.' Make time, find the money. Even brisk walking is better than nothing – much better than nothing!

Sleep. When we lose sleep we become more emotional, less rational and less effective. You can see how this alone can contribute to stress and anger. Treat seriously any sleeping problems that you have, and take positive action to problem-solve them. There is plenty of help available at the click of a button on the internet.

Relaxation. Being stressed is exhausting – physically, mentally and emotionally. So we need to make sure that we build some relaxation into our lives. This is true even when we are not stressed, so all the more true when we are! Regular relaxation reduces tension and blood pressure, both of which are symptoms of stress.

Attending to your breathing is an extremely effective way of relaxing. You may already have used breathing to turn the heat down on your anger. When we go into fight or flight mode, we start breathing in a very shallow way, or even stop breathing altogether, in preparation for action. Reversing this process has immediate physiological effects. A few deep breaths from the belly (not from the chest) will give powerful messages to the brain that you are calming down, and so will actually calm you down. (See also page 53 above.)

The more you practise breathing on a day to day basis, when you are relatively relaxed, the more it will help you when you are in the depths of a stress response. It's not so effective starting to breathe deeply only as an emergency measure.

There are many simple relaxation techniques (see Fig. 9.3). Key to all of them is to practise them. You need to build relaxation into your life, not snatch it once or twice when particularly stressed.

FIND A PLACE WHERE YOU WILL NOT BE DISTURBED. LIE DOWN OR SIT IN A COMFORTABLE POSITION AND CLOSE YOUR EYES.

TENSE AND RELAX YOUR MUSCLES IN GROUPS, E.G. (I) THE HEAD, FACE, NECK AND SHOULDERS, (II) THE CHEST, ARMS AND BACK, (III) THE BUTTOCKS, LEGS AND FEET. TENSE EACH GROUP IN TURN FOR ABOUT 10 SECONDS, THEN RELAX IT AND NOTICE THE DIFFERENCE.

ONCE YOU ARE PHYSICALLY RELAXED, FOCUS ON YOUR BREATHING – IN THROUGH THE NOSE AND OUT THROUGH THE MOUTH. LET YOUR BREATHING COME FROM THE STOMACH RATHER THAN THE CHEST.

SAY A NUMBER IN YOUR MIND EACH TIME YOU BREATHE OUT. THIS 'MANTRA' HELPS TO STOP UNHELPFUL THOUGHTS DISTURBING YOU. WHEN YOUR MIND WANDERS, BRING IT BACK GENTLY TO FOCUS ON YOUR BREATHING.

DO THIS FOR ANYTHING BETWEEN 5 AND 20 MINUTES.

COME BACK INTO THE PRESENT SLOWLY.

Fig. 9.3 A simple relaxation technique

DO IT!

For one week, practise the relaxation technique described in the flowchart for 15 minutes every day. Record the difference that it makes to your levels of stress-related feeling.

Diet. The things we put into ourselves can be key stressors (a stressor is something that causes stress). It may be tempting to reach for a cigarette when you are stressed, because you associate it with calming yourself. Actually studies have shown that smoking increases people's stress. This is because of the chemicals it releases into the bloodstream, the physical ill-health that it causes, and the added stimulation that smoking gives to an already over-stimulated system.

In addition, smoking covers up the main reason why we are getting stressed (whatever that is), so it doesn't allow us to problem-solve.

The same applies to alcohol, caffeine, drugs and junk food. Check out how all of these substances are stressors by searching on the internet.

DO
IT !

Think about your own physical responses to stress and how you can make changes to break the cycle. Draw up a stress management plan like the one below:

Stress management action plan: 1 Physical

ACTION TO BE TAKEN	START DATE	REVIEW DATE

CHANGE YOUR BEHAVIOUR

Work-related stress. Overwork usually results in stress. Think about your work practices. Are you able to say 'No' when the workload or deadlines become too demanding? Are you able to ask for help or delegate? If not, then re-read chapter 8, as you may need to work on your assertiveness.

You may be overworking to avoid problems in other areas of your life. Be honest with yourself. Is avoidance going to make the problems better or worse? Effectively you are using work as an alcoholic uses another pint of beer, to blot out the pain. You know in your heart of hearts that it makes the issue even harder to tackle, but no less urgent.

Work-life balance has become a cliché, which means it has less power as an idea any more. We say, 'Oh, yeah, work-life balance – that would be nice.' But a balanced lifestyle is essential, and an unbalanced lifestyle is a key stressor. We may feel the adrenalin buzz for working 12-hour days, but when the chemicals have done their job we also feel worn out, resentful at 'having' to work so hard, and unfulfilled in our relationships and personal lives.

copymaster 79

DO IT! Think about the things that you do regularly for yourself outside work. These could be active, such as sport; solitary, such as fixing bikes; or involve friends. If you are not doing enough to 'feed yourself' in this way, ask yourself why not. Don't allow yourself to get away with excuses – you have a choice here. Make a positive choice to resume something you have stopped doing, or take up something new. What's the first step that you need to take to make that choice real? Take that step.

Time management. Men who feel they do not have enough hours in the day are often stressed. Sometimes simple time management skills can help, such as making a list of important tasks at the beginning of the week, prioritising them, and checking/revising the list daily. Or you may be a 'Type A' male – high-achieving, competitive, but also impatient and hurried. Questioning your assumptions and basic beliefs will help you slow down a bit (see next section).

Procrastination, or putting off tasks, is a good example of a behavioural response to stress that increases rather than decreases our stress levels. The graph in Fig. 9.4 shows how this works. Stress levels rise as you realise that there is an important and/or difficult task to do. To make you feel better, you put the task off and do other things instead. This lowers your stress level temporarily, until you realise that not only haven't you done the task, now you have even less time to complete it properly. And so the cycle continues, ratcheting up the stress.

copymaster 80

copymaster 81

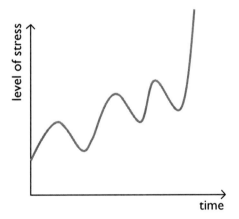

Fig. 9.4 The relationship between procrastination and levels of stress

If you procrastinate then you will also be doing irrelevant things such as unimportant tasks, surfing the net or watching TV programmes you don't enjoy. These are called displacement activities. Watch out for them and don't kid yourself that they are doing you any good.

Steve was a popular head of department in a secondary school, but found himself leaving important paperwork and lesson preparation until the very last minute. Sometimes he would work all night; at other times he would phone in sick so as not to face the music. He realised that his 'displacement activity' – surfing the internet – was adding further problems to his life. His action plan for change included three key tools: he stayed for an hour after school to complete important work, he stuck a poster by his desk at work which said JUST DO IT!, and he began to address his fear of failure (see chapter 7 above).

Think about your own behavioural responses to stress and how you can make changes to break the cycle. Draw up a stress management plan like the one below:

Stress management action plan: 2 Behavioural

ACTION TO BE TAKEN	START DATE	REVIEW DATE

CHANGE YOUR THINKING

Thinking patterns. Stress guru Stephen Palmer defines stress as occurring 'when perceived pressure exceeds your perceived ability to cope'. Note that repeated word 'perceived'. It takes us right to the heart of the problem of stress – that stress is born and bred in the mind. Yes, there are situations that are notoriously more likely to result in stress (divorce, moving house …). However, what actually causes the stress is the way in which we interpret those situations.

Think about it – if overwork *caused* stress then any busy employee, from junior doctor to chief executive of a transnational organisation, would by definition be stressed.

This is good news, because it means the biggest tool we have to get on top of our stress lies within ourselves. We need to identify our unhelpful patterns of thinking and adjust them.

The angry, stressed men that I see get hooked into one (or more) of these thinking patterns:

> ***must-itis*** – when we use too many musts and shoulds. This sets up rigid rules for our behaviour. Telling ourselves that 'I must get that promotion by such and such a date' or 'She must respond to my email in such and such terms' builds up the pressure of huge expectations for yourself and others. Challenge such inflexible beliefs. Give yourself (and others) some slack. You will not be throwing your standards out of the window, simply adjusting them for the benefit of all concerned. (See also pages 84-85 above.)

> ***catastrophising*** – imagining and predicting the worst. This again heightens our stress response. Remember that the stress reaction is set off in the first place by our perception of danger. If we then imagine the worst, we are going to be even more in danger! So it's important that we catch ourselves catastrophising and challenge these anxious predictions at source. Develop a calm and reasonable 'inner dialogue' instead (see chapter 5).

copymaster 83

I-can't-stand-it-itis – thinking that we can't bear the situation, or specifically that we 'can't cope'. This is a form of catastrophising, because if we really can't bear it, then what …? Will we go mad? Collapse? In fact usually we can bear it and we can cope, as long as we focus on what we can do about the situation in a calm, problem-solving way. Underestimating our resources to cope actually undermines those resources.

When you notice that you are catastrophising, ask yourself these questions:
- 'What evidence is there that this will actually happen?'
- 'What else could happen?'
- 'What is likely to happen?'
- 'If the worst actually did happen, what could I do about it?'

Assumptions. Angry, stressed men can also base their thinking and behaviour on some deeper level assumptions, or rules of behaviour, about themselves and the world. These assumptions may also need challenging.

One common assumption that I come across is 'The world is against me.' If you perceive that life is a constant battle and that you have to be on your guard against attack, this is exhausting and stressful. You will also see evidence everywhere to 'fit' your assumption. If life is a battle zone, that may be because you have turned it into one. You are almost certainly in danger of personalising (see page 63 above). Try to view people and events more objectively and compassionately.

Ross seemed to be permanently stressed and angry. For example he would step out of the way of people on the pavement, then complain that they never did that for him. A friend pointed this out, asking, 'How can they do it for you when you always do it first?' He experimented with holding his ground on the pavement, and was shocked to see how people willingly stepped aside for him. He began to recognise how he expected the worst in people, and how unhelpful that was. He linked it in with his fear of criticism, and worked on building up his self-esteem.

Another assumption that men have is that they 'have to' respond to any incident that involves them. There may be potential 'loss of face' here (see chapter 7) that needs addressing. But it may also just be a habit.

Let me share a personal anecdote. I stepped out of my door one day and nearly had a collision with a young man cycling on the pavement. Just as I was puffing myself up to bellow angrily at him, he turned and said, 'Don't pick it up, mate,' before disappearing round the corner. His remark completely deflated me, but I was also really amused and relieved. I realised that he was right: I didn't have to pick it up. Sure, he shouldn't have been cycling on the pavement, but no damage was done. Would it have made my life better by getting into an angry strop about it?

Ask yourself if you 'have to' react in an angry or stressed way to an unexpected incident. Just say to yourself, 'Don't pick it up!' and move on.

Using humour. Often our stressed, angry reactions come from taking ourselves too seriously. Be honest – many of the incidents that wind you up and 'cause' stress-related anger are actually the same incidents that you laugh about with your mates in the pub a day or two later. So if you can choose to see the funny side of the situation then, why not at the time? It is a choice, after all, even if it's one that needs practising.

The next time you feel like exploding with stress, think how you would relate the incident in a funny way to your friends. Explode with laughter instead. It has been scientifically proved that laughter is hugely beneficial to your health – and that stress isn't.

copymaster 85

DO IT! Identify your own thinking responses to stress and how you can make changes to break the cycle. Draw up a stress management plan like the one below:

copymaster 86

Stress management action plan: 3 Thinking skills

ACTION TO BE TAKEN	START DATE	REVIEW DATE

TOOLKIT

- Recognise the signs and symptoms of stress, and make a commitment to tackling the issue. Remember that stress is a response to events, and that you have responsibility for your responses.
- Make sure you take regular exercise, and build relaxation into your daily life.
- Check out your diet for stressors such as caffeine, junk food and alcohol.
- Address work-related stress in a problem-solving way. In particular, assess whether your life is too work-oriented.
- Attend to your time management skills by prioritising your key tasks and addressing procrastination.
- Notice and challenge stress-related thinking patterns such as must-itis, catastrophising and I-can't-stand-it-itis.
- Challenge some basic assumptions that cause stress, such as 'The world is against me' and 'I have to react here.'
- Laugh at yourself and situations – it's a great stress buster.
- Draw up a comprehensive stress management action plan, covering your physical, behavioural and psychological responses to stress. Review at regular intervals.

learning log

WHAT I HAVE LEARNT	WHAT I CAN DO

| # MY ANGER TOOLKIT

copymaster 89

Whatever you have learnt about yourself and your anger while reading this book, it is vital that you keep your learning going. One way of doing this is to draw up your own personal toolkit or action plan to summarise what you have learnt and remind yourself of the key tools that you can use in future to manage your anger or irritation.

You could draw up a sheet like the one below:

MY ANGER TOOLKIT

It is understandable that I have been an angry man because:
[list any life experiences, role models etc that have contributed to the development of your anger]

However, getting too angry has the following consequences:
[list consequences to your health, relationships, self-esteem, effectiveness etc.]

I have to take responsibility for my anger. That means noticing the key triggers, such as:
[list key triggers for your anger]

It helps to notice when I'm getting more angry than I need to. The symptoms I have to look out for are:
[list the warning signs you notice in yourself, e.g. heart racing, raised voice, particular unhelpful thinking styles]

The key tools I use to turn the heat down on my anger are:
[list your 5 or 6 key tools here – cover thinking tools, behaviour tools, physical(body) tools]

- Read this summary regularly
-
-

-
-
-

APPENDIX 2 | TO THE PARTNER IN YOUR LIFE

Living with an angry and aggressive man is really hard. Take heart from the fact that your partner is reading this book. That means he has begun to own up that he is angry. And that this needs fixing. And – crucially – that he is the one who must fix it.

Because up to now, he has probably blamed others – other people, other things – for his anger instead of taking responsibility. And 'other people' often means those closest to him. The people who see him at his most vulnerable. The people who can push his buttons. People like you.

But it is essential that you do not take the blame for his anger. There may be things you do that trigger his anger, but that is entirely different. Maybe you don't say the 'right' thing, or do the 'right' thing. You have to take responsibility for your actions, of course, but he has to take responsibility for his reaction to your actions.

So how can you help your man fix his anger problem?

Hand the problem over to him.

However much he may blame you, say, 'You have chosen to be angry. I am not responsible for your anger.'

Remember that his anger will often be a cover for more difficult feelings or 'weaknesses', such as low self-esteem. So boost his self-confidence where you can.

Remember that it is possible to change behaviour, however deeply engrained. Reading this book is one step on that journey.

Draw a line at his violence and abuse. He must hear that this is totally unacceptable.

Keep yourself and your children safe. Use these support services:

- National Domestic Violence Helpline (UK) (0808 2000 247). A 24 hour freephone helpline run by Women's Aid and Refuge which provides refuge, information and counselling for victims of domestic violence.
- The Broken Rainbow helpline (UK) (08452 604460) is a specialist service for gay and transgender people experiencing domestic violence.
- National Domestic Violence Hotline (USA) is available 24 hours a day, every day (1–800–799–SAFE (7233) or TTY 1–800–787–3224), assistance in English or Spanish.

Books

The best full-length book on anger that I have come across is from the USA: *Beyond Anger: A guide for men* by Thomas J. Harbin (Marlowe & Company, 2000). It is thoughtful, well written, rooted in clinical (and personal) experience, and based on the same cognitive behavioural principles as the FIX IT series of books.

Find Your Power by Dr Chris Johnstone (Nicholas Brealey, 2006) is an inspirational manual to help anyone make positive changes in their lives, and can therefore be used alongside the present book.

For assertiveness problems I would recommend *Assertiveness at Work* by Ken Back and Kate Back (2nd edn McGraw-Hill, 1991). This appears to be out of print, so please buy a second hand copy from Amazon or another supplier!

If your anger stems from issues of self-esteem, read (and use) *Zero to Hero: From cringing to confident in 100 steps* by Christine Wilding and Stephen Palmer (Hodder Arnold, 2006). Despite the fun approach and lively design of this book, it is a practical and effective toolbox of techniques that many of my own clients have benefited from reading.

If stress is your main problem, then try *How to Deal with Stress* by Stephen Palmer and Cary Cooper (Kogan Page, 2007).

Organisations and websites

The *Everyman Project* (UK) is a charitable organisation based in London which offers a range of support services for men who want to stop behaving violently or abusively, and for the people affected by their violence or abuse. These include a focused brief counselling programme, a partner support programme, and a telephone help-line (0207 263 8884). http://www.everymanproject.co.uk/

The *Respect Phoneline* (0845 122 8609) (UK) is a helpline offering information and advice to people who want to stop being abusive towards their partners. http://www.respectphoneline.org.uk

The mental health charity *Mind* (UK) has a website full of helpful information and advice about all sorts of emotional issues that may underlie and/or accompany anger. There is also a confidential helpline which provides information (0845 766 0163). http://www.mind.org.uk/

The *British Association of Anger Management* (UK) offers workshops, courses, counselling, training and information. http://www.angermanage.co.uk/

Therapeutic help

Anger management courses are everywhere. There are even some that you can do online. Just type 'anger management' and your nearest large town into Google.

Sometimes the issues may seem too big for you to grapple with on your own. You may need to work with a trained *therapist, counsellor, psychologist or psychotherapist*. Ask your GP for a recommendation, or search for one yourself online, e.g. http://www.bacp.co.uk/ – click on 'Find a Therapist' (UK) or http://www.individual.therapists.net/ (US). Phone several therapists and discuss your needs. Meet at least two for an initial assessment session – remember that you are assessing them as well as the other way round. If you like the principles and methods adopted in this book, make sure that your chosen therapist uses a cognitive behavioural approach (CBT, REBT and others). Do not expect to sort your problems out overnight. Do not expect your therapist to do the work for you.

Here's a checklist of questions to ask yourself when you challenge any thought or series of thoughts that is causing you to get angry.

Identify the key thought (NAT) and ask yourself:

- Am I jumping to conclusions?
- Am I mind reading? How do I know they are thinking that?
- Is my view is the only possible one? (What other views of this event could people hold?)
- Am I paying attention only to the negative side of things?
- Am I overestimating the chances of disaster?
- Am I exaggerating the importance of events?
- Am I assuming that I can't do anything to alter this situation? (What can I realistically do?)
- Am I expecting myself or others to be perfect?
- Am I using a double standard?
- Am I totally condemning someone (or myself) on the basis of a single event?
- Am I fretting about how things should be rather than dealing with them as they are?
- Am I blaming myself for something that isn't my fault?
- Am I thinking in all or nothing (black and white) terms?
- Am I using ultimatum words (should/must/have to)?
- Am I taking things personally that have little or nothing to do with me?
- Am I predicting the outcome and assuming it will be terrible?

1 *Prepare your script*

Follow these four steps: Explanation, Feelings, Needs, Consequences. (Remember the mnemonic – Even Fish Need Confidence.)

- **Explanation** – explain the situation as you see it. Be brief, objective and keep to the point.
- **Feelings** – acknowledge your feelings and take responsibility for them (say 'I'm fed up that...' not 'You make me fed up'). Acknowledging the other's feelings as well can help (see technique 2 below).
- **Needs** – say clearly and calmly what you want out of the situation.
- **Consequences** – say what will happen as a result (rewards, benefits, punishments) but don't indulge in empty threats.

2 *Show that you understand the other person's position*

Before you state what you feel or need, it is really helpful to empathise with the other person. It shows them that you understand their own feelings, or the situation they are in. Say things like this:

I know that you must be fed up ... but ...

I understand that you are in a difficult position ... but ...

I can see that you are busy ... but ...

I realise you don't like doing the washing up ... but ...

3 *Be prepared to negotiate*

Assertiveness does not mean that you must get your way at all costs. It often results in some sort of compromise or negotiation. Sometimes a compromise is the only way forward, so that both parties' rights are respected. A compromise can be a win-win situation.

Don't be stubborn and wait for the other to 'give in'. Negotiating is not a 'loss of face'. It is often the most sensible and realistic option, with the best outcome for both parties.

4 Broken record

The broken record technique is used when we need to stick to our message, despite all interruptions, put-downs, diversions and attempts to rile us. You simply repeat the same message, calmly and clearly. Here, for example, Jim is asserting his right to explain why he is late home:

Jim: *The phone rang just as I was leaving the office …*
Sue: That's what you always say. I've been worried sick …
Jim: *I would like to finish my explanation please.*
Sue: It's only an excuse. You don't care about anything or anyone. You …
Jim: *Sue, I would like to finish my explanation.*
Sue: How long is this going to take? We're late already.
Jim: *As I was saying, I was leaving the office when …*

5 Communicate clearly

When you communicate your opinion, whether it is a complaint, a compliment or whatever, make sure you do this clearly and directly.

- State what you mean – don't beat about the bush.
- Be concise – get to the point
- Don't feel you have to fill in any silences – let the other person do that if they want to

Above all, **don't lose your temper**, because this will not result in clear communication, only escalation of any conflict. If you feel yourself losing control, take some deep breaths and count to 10 before speaking. You cannot be assertive if you are aggressive.

6 *Take responsibility*

Commit to the point you want to make and take full responsibility for it.

- That means saying things like, 'I think that …' rather than 'We think that …'
- Don't say, 'You make me feel …', but 'I feel …'
- Don't make personal references like 'You are really irritating'. Instead say, 'I am irritated when …'

7 *Only apologise when you need to*

- Don't apologise before or after you speak, e.g. 'I'm really sorry but …' This undermines you. You don't have to apologise for expressing your feelings respectfully!
- On the other hand, it is fine and even helpful to apologise for things that you feel you should have done differently, e.g. 'I should have warned you, that's true, but I'm not happy that …'

8 *Use effective verbal and body language*

- Practise speaking in a clear, firm voice, without raising your tone or mumbling or trembling.
- Likewise be aware of your body language. Stand or sit an appropriate distance away, face the person you are speaking to and maintain eye contact.

9 *Check you have been heard*

You may need to check that you have been listened to. You could ask for the person to summarise what you have said so that it's absolutely clear. Don't allow them to make the excuse that they misheard or misunderstood you.

10 Stick to the facts

- Don't make things up to strengthen your case. It's important to be truthful.
- Likewise don't speak in exaggerated or emotional language. It's much more effective to be objective and rational.

'You always leave your clothes all over the floor. It's a nightmare – it takes me hours to put them away' is exaggerated and emotional. It won't gain respect and is easy to deny.

'When you leave your clothes on the floor like this, I feel a bit cross because ...' is probably much truer and certainly more effective.

Breinigsville, PA USA
29 September 2010
246379BV00003B/28/P

9 780956 407603